Italy, Perugia Travel Guide, Italy

Italy, Umbria, Perugia Tour

Author
Caleb Gray.

Publisher:
SONITTEC LTD
College House, 2nd
Floor
17 King Edwards
Road,
Ruislip
London
HA4 7AE.

Table of Content

Summary

The importance of travelling in our life?
Everyone has their very own reasons to travel.
Some people travel for work, some travel for pleasure while for others it is just a way of life. They travel to live and to escape at the same time.

Whatever might be the reason to travel, here are few ways in which travelling would definitely change you and I think that is why travelling becomes so important in life:

Enjoy being alone: There is something therapeutic about being alone and being at peace with it.

While you soak in a new culture, you also connect with your own inner self.

<u>Learn to adapt</u>: It is a different world out there, literally. Be it the pace of life, the language or simply the change in weather, it is always a change and you have to adapt to it. This is what makes travelling truly beautiful as you break away from the routine and adapt to something totally new.

<u>Experience a new culture</u>: Every place comes with its distinct cultural habits, you cannot think about New York without talking about its fast paced life and about Italy without enjoying its relaxed lifestyle. Similarly, while visiting the UK you might have to be a bit formal in your interactions with the locals, on the other hand, while greeting the people in Thailand, one can be really warm and casual.

<u>Broaden your taste buds</u>: Travelling without experiencing the local food is just not complete. It is not only a culinary experience but a cultural one as well.

<u>Get out of comfort zone</u>: From simple experiences like the weather, way of life or food to the more adventurous ones like trying a new sport, travelling really pushes ones boundaries to the core. You might end up participating in a street carnival in Brazil just like the locals or trying the local delicacies (read insects) in Thailand.

<u>Indulge in Photography</u>: It does not matter whether you are a professional or not. It is also irrelevant whether you have a DSLR or a very basic camera, while travelling what matters is the love and quest for seeing beautiful places and the sheer joy of capturing them in your lense. Travelling would in return give you your very own collection

of amazing postcards of beautiful sunsets, snow laced mountains or sunny beaches.

Learn to escape: Travelling is the best way to break the routine. If you are in a bustling city, go ahead and experience the country life. If you are in a rural place, travel to a bustling city and experience its madness. Stressed with the city life or work pressure? A spa break in Himalayas or Kerala is a must try.

Appreciate Nature: The quest to explore more when one is travelling always leads to a sense of amazement about nature. While most of us keep a track of technological advancements, Nature has its own ways of outshining all of these. The Antelope Canyon in Arizona or Turquoise Ice in Russia are the finest examples of this. For more, check out the most unbelievable places around the world.

<u>Get closer to your own roots</u>: While one travels and experiences a lot of different cultures and practices, it definitely brings one closer to his or her own roots. Travel helps one appreciate one's identity and culture.

Travelling is all about experiences. They can happen in terms of culture, people, places but most importantly with one's own self and this was all about

History of Umbria

The history of Umbria overlaps somewhat with it's better known neighbor Tuscany in the eras of the Etruscans and the Romans, but it has also forged it's own footprints in Italian history throughout the ages. The first two major groups to share Umbria were the Umbri and the Etruscans. Although the Etruscans are better known, the Umbri settled the region first, it is said as far back as 672 BC, which is the date of origin of the town of Terni, which was then called Interamna. At that time, the language was Umbrian, a relative of Latin and Oscan. Archaeological evidence shows that the Umbri can be identified with the creators of the Terramara, and probably also of the Villanovan culture in northern and central Italy, who at the beginning of the Bronze Age displaced the original Ligurian population by an invasion from the north-east. The Apennine civilization occupied Umbria's hills and mountains and lived off agriculture and animals. There are many remnants left behind from this time including decorated vases, and many tools of stone, bone and metal.

The Etruscans were chief enemies of the Umbri, and the Etruscan invasion went from the western seaboard towards the north and east (lasting from about 700 to 500 BC), eventually driving the Umbrians towards the Apenninic uplands and capturing 300 Umbrian towns. The river Tiber, Tevere in Italian, mostly divided the two populations with the Umbri on the east, and the Etruscan on the west. The Umbri tribe flourished early on in eastern towns such as Spoleto, Gubbio,

Città di Castello and Assisi. Etruscans established towns we know today as Perugia, Orvieto and Città della Pieve, eventually creating 12 powerful city-states. Traces of this past can still be seen in the excellent Museo Archeologico Nazionale dell'Umbria in Perugia. What little is known about the Umbri from this time comes from the famous Eugubine Tablets in Gubbio. These seven bronze slabs were written in the 2nd century BC in the Umbrian language. They describer religious rites as well as the political system of that time.

Things seriously changed in Umbria around 300 BC when soldiers from Rome arrived. In 295 BC, Rome conquered the Etruscans, and all of their lands, including Umbria, fell under Roman rule. Despite the legendary Roman plundering and pillaging, the Romans actually had a positive influence on Umbria as they initiated public works that are still visible to this day. Emperor Gaius Flaminius built the Via Flaminia in 220 BC, a road which connected Rome to Ancona and the Adriatic Sea, and passed through towns such as Narni, Terni, Spoleto and Foligno, all of which are still littered with Roman ruins. A minor road branched off to Perugia, whose prominence as the capital of Umbria was growing. In 90 BC, Umbrians were granted full Roman citizenship and, for a handful of centuries, the region thrived.

After Rome fell, invasions by Saracens, Goths, Lombards, Byzantines and the barbarians led to an economic and cultural decline in Umbria. Starvation and disease were rampant, and Umbrians retreated to fortified medieval hill towns such as Gubbio and Todi. Conditions were perfect for the new Roman cult of Christianity to flourish. The church of Sant'Angelo in Perugia, built over a former pagan temple around the 5th and 6th centuries AD, is one of Italy's oldest extant churches outside of Rome.

The political power gap during the Middle Ages was quickly filled by the Lombard Duchy of Spoleto from the 6th to the 13th centuries, until Umbria became a papal territory. Prominent Umbrian families tended to favor rule by either the pope or the Holy Roman Empire, creating a split between Guelphs, or papal supporters, and Ghibellines, those who followed the emperors. Spoleto and Todi became Ghibelline cities while Perugia and Orvieto, which both benefited initially from Papal rule, became Guelph cities. The remnants of the conflict still dot Umbria today in the form of the rocca, or Papal fortress, examples of which can be seen in Perugia, Assisi and Narni.

Many important saints, such as Benedict of Norcia who became the patron of Europe, had put Umbria on the mystical map, but it was in the 13th century when Umbria's most famous son, St Francis of Assisi was born, that cemented Umbria's reputation as a centre for spirituality, which continues to this day.

The province of Umbria was created in 1861 as part of a unified region. At that time Umbria included the current provinces of Terni and Perugia as well as Rieti. At this time though, the economic situation of the region was in grave danger as agriculture was languishing and farmers were forced to move to other areas to feed their families. During the industrial revolution, Umbria began to rebuild once the railway line was built linking Rome, Terni, and Foligno in 1866. World War Two followed this slight economic growth and many industries were bombed resulting in in a slow postwar recovery.

Historians of Umbrian culture like to say that time stopped in 1544 when the pope installed a salt tax, resulting in a Salt War that caused a standstill in Umbrian culture. It is felt because of this, that the Renaissance didn't flourish in Umbria like it did in neighboring Tuscany. To this day, Umbria still retains much of its ancient history as seen when visiting its many hill towns spread across the region, and time seems to move a little slower here in Umbria, even for visitors.

Touristic Introduction of Perugia

Perugia is one of the most attractive towns in the area of northern Umbria and southern Tuscany, Italy, both in terms of its ambience and its art, architecture and history. Perugia should on no account be missed if you are visiting central Italy. Perhaps nowhere else in Italy are the material remains of the Etruscans so clearly evident as in this city. The churches and fountain of the main piazza are well-known masterpieces, but there are numerous minor churches of great interest, most notably the Tempio di San Michele Arcangelo.

Within easy reach of Perugia, there are a number of hill towns in Umbria that are worth a visit. One example is Corciano, a small mediaeval town situated on a hill 5 miles from Perugia, on a detour of the road to Lake Trasimeno. Corciano was under the rule of Perugia until the 16 C, when it was annexed to the Papal State and became Corgna family's domain. Corciano is surrounded by a fine circuit of walls and fortified towers and the splendid castle dominates the maze of narrow alleys and flights of steps that connect the piazzas and their beautiful architecture. Some of the public buildings have spectacular interior decoration.

Perugia: Piazza IV Novembre
The Piazza IV Novembre forms the centre of Perugia which speads outwards along the steep alleys leading to the walls of the original Etruscan settlement and the ancient gates of Porta Marzia,

Porta Sole, Porta Cornea, Porta Trasimena, Porta della Mandorla and the Arco Etrusco. The piazza is one of the most beautiful squares in Umbria, indeed, in all of Italy, surrounded as it is by fine buildings.

Perugia: Fontana Maggiore
Fontana Maggiore is located at the centre of Piazza IV Novembre. This beautiful mediaeval fountain was erected in the second half of the 12 C at the termination of the aqueduct that carried water to the town from Monte Pacciano. The architect was Fra Bevignate da Perugia and the sculptural decorations were created by Nicola and Giovanni Pisano. The fountain is composed of two superimposed polygonal basins, faced with marble reliefs representing biblical and mythological individuals, saints, animals and personifications of the months, the sciences, the virtues and places. The fountain is one of the finest examples of

Gothic art in Italy and was the symbol of the city at the peak of its power and influence.

Perugia: Cathedral of San Lorenzo

The work of building the Cathedral of San Lorenzo took more than a century, finishing at the end of 1400s. The left side, facing the square, has a bronze statue of Julius III, the portal by Ippolito Scalza, and large Gothic windows, plus the elegant arches of the Loggia di Braccio, erected in 1423. Under the portico there is a section of the Roman walls, the base of the old bell-tower and a copy of the Pietra della Giustizia (Stone of Justice), a document of the Comune dating back to 1200. The façade of the church, facing onto Piazza Danti, was remodelled in Baroque style. The interior, divided into three naves, contains distinguished works of art, including the Cappella del Santo Anello, preserving, according to tradition, the ring of the Virgin, the Cappella di San Bernardino; the very fine choir stalls by Giuliano da Maiano and Domenico del Tasso.

Perugia: Palazzo dei Priori and Sala dei Notari

Another side of the square is occupied by the Palazzo dei Priori, which was the residence of the principal political authorities of the city during the Middle Ages. Construction was begun in 1298 and the work was completed in 1353. The palace is built of travertine and red and white stone from Bettona, and on the side facing the fountain it has a large stairway and a portal which gives access to the beautiful Sala dei Notari, a rectangular room with a vault supported by huge Romanesque arches and walls covered with frescoes. The façade has two lines of mullioned windows with three lights and a portico.

The side of the palace facing onto Corso Vannucci has an undulating development and is characterised by mullioned windows with three and four lights, and a magnificent round portal. The interior of the Palazzo dei Priori comprises the National Gallery of Umbria the most important collection of art in Umbria for the Mediaeval and the Modern periods and, on the ground floor level, the Sala del Collegio del Cambio and the Sala del Collegio della Mercanzia. The Guild of Merchants established its seat in this palace in 1390 and decorated their meeting room with wooden panels, a very unusual decoration, rather rare in Italy. The Guild of Moneychangers occupied this wing of the palace during the half of the 15 C. in this room can be admired the most important work by Perugino in Perugia, one of the most significant examples of Renaissance painting in Italy: a series of frescoes representing the heroes and deities of antiquity and some personified virtues.

Perugia: Basilica of San Domenico

The Basilica of San Domenico, a massive structure, was erected, according to Vasari, by Giovanni Pisano in the 1304 in the place where, in the Middle Ages, the market and the horse fair were held, and where the Dominicans settled in 1234. Around the 1614 the vaults and pillars of the nave collapsed and after the reconstruction by Carlo Madeno of Rome, the church was re consecrated in the 1632. Inside, there are Gothic elements, renaissance windows and the tomb of Pope Benedetto XI. The Archaeological Museum of the Umbria and the State Archives are housed in the adjacent monastery and cloister.

Perugia: Church of San Pietro
The Church of San Pietro, a Benedictine abbey, was founded in the 10 C on the Monte Calvario. It functioned as the cathedral of Perugia in the 6 C (located outside the town walls at that time), prior to the status of cathedral being given to Santo

Stefano in Castellare (demolished during the construction of the abbey and church of San Domenico) around 936 and then finally to San Lorenzo, the current cathedral.

The triple-arched portal at the entrance to the main court reflects Porta di San Pietro, which is visible from here. It was built in 1614 to a design by Valentino Martelli, who had also designed the main cloister and a second foor that was never built.

Church of San Pietro
The minor cloister (or 'delle Stelle'), was designed by Galeazzo Alessi in 1571. The main court is dominated by the polygonal clock-tower, supposedly built on the site of an Etruscan tomb that was used for its construction in the 13 C. After a partial collapse, the upper section was rebuilt in 1463 to plans by Bernardo Rossellino.

The interior is a mixture of ancient columns and has a Palaeochristian basilical structure. The Gothic wooden choir is considered to be one of the finest in Italy and was completed between 1525 and 1591. The painted and guilded wooden lacunar ceiling is from 1556, while the large quantity of frescos and paintings by various artists include some by Antonio Vassillacchi (1592-94), Sassoferrato, Guido Reni, Vasari, Guerricino and Perugino (Pietro Vannucci).

The sacristy was added in 1451 and contains inlaid furnishings from 1472, as well as the remains of a pavement in Deruta tiles. The frescoes are by Danti and Peccenini. The paintings hanging here are by Perugino, Parmigianino and Raphael. A door in the apse of the wooden choir leads to a tiny balcony that affords a stunning view over the Valle Umbra as far as Assisi, Monte Subasio, Bettona, Montefalco and the Apennines.

The buildings of the abbey around the two cloisters now house the Agriculture Faculty of the University of Perugia, which also owns the abbey's former properties in Casalina, in the Tiber valley.

History of Perugia

Perugia is a substantial town located in Umbria, central Italy, on a hill on the right of the Tiber. The Gothic cathedral is of the 14 C, but its façade is still unfinished. The cathedral contains paintings by Baroccio, Manni and Signorelli. It houses a marble sarcophagus containing the remains of Pope Urban IV and Pope Martin IV. An onyx ring is preserved, traditionally the marriage ring of Mary, in the chapel del Santo Anello. This ring was venerated first at Chiusi, whence it was stolen in the 15 C and taken to Perugia. In the chapter library a 6 C codex of the Gospel of St. Luke is preserved. Other churches in Perugia are: San Pietro dei Cassinesi, the church of a monastery founded by St. Peter Vincioli about 1000; San Ercolano, the high altar of which is made of an ancient sarcophagus; Sant' Angelo, a round building, dating from the 6 C; the Madonna della Luce, a graceful little temple by Galeazzo Alessio; San Francesco del Prato, now the seat of the Accademia of fine arts.

The university, founded in 1320, has three faculties, and contains a museum of Etruscan, Roman and Christian antiquities, with many sculptures and inscriptions. Among the latter is the "Tabulæ Perusinæ", discovered in 1822.

The most notable ancient monuments of the town are the Porta Augusta, the tomb of the Volumnii, which was discovered in 1840 by Vermiglioli, and the Etruscan walls.

Perugia from the Etruscans to Middle Ages

Perugia was among the most important cities of the Etruscans, with whom it took part in the wars against Rome in 310 and 295 B.C., and also in the Samnite War. The Perugian War (41 B.C.) is famous - the troops of Mark Anthony were besieged and compelled to surrender. During the Gothic War, Perugia suffered various sieges - by the Byzantines in 537 and 552, and by the Goths in 546 and 548. The Lombards had taken possession of the city at the time of their first incursion, but in 592 it again came under Byzantine rule and was made the seat of a Dux. In 749, it was besieged by the Lombard King Rachis, who, however, was persuaded by Pope Zacharias to raise the siege. Pepin gave the city to the Holy See. From the beginning of the 11 C, Perugia was established as a free commune and was periodically involved in conflicts with the neighbouring cities of Umbria and of Tuscany (Chiusi, 1012; Cortona, 1049; Assisi, 1054; Todi,

1056; Foligno, 1080 and 1090). It was governed by consuls who were later by the Priori delle Arti in 1303. After 1174, there was a podestà, and later a capitano del popolo.

Perugia and the Papacy

Perugia was friendly to Florence and faithful to the Holy See, and was essentially a Guelph city. In the 13 C, the popes established their residence here for a long time. Four of them were elected here (Pope Honorius III, Pope Honorius IV, Pope Celestine V, and Pope Clement V). On the other hand, continuing its wars with neighbouring cities (Spoleto, from 1324, was besieged for two years), Perugia extended its sovereignty over the greater portion of Umbria, and over a part of Tuscany. In 1375 it was among the first cities that revolted against Pope Gregory IX at the instance of the Florentines. Meanwhile, two parties had been formed: the Raspanti (the popular party) and the

Beccarini (the party of the nobles), and between them they had made it possible for Biondo Michelotti to become lord of the city in 1390.

He, however, was killed in 1393, and then Gian Galeazzo Visconti took possession of the town, but in 1403 it became subject to Pope Boniface IX. Afterwards it fell into the power of Ladislao di Napoli. In 1416 the city was taken by Braccio da Montone, who was recognized as lord of Perugia by Pope Martin V. At his death in 1424, the nobles came into power, but contention soon developed among them, and eventually the Baglioni made away with the Oddi family. Finally, Gian Paolo Baglione became a tyrant of the city, making himself detested by his cruelty and dissolute habits. He was brought under control in 1506 by Pope Julius II, but fresh cruelties against his own relations led to his decapitation by order of Pope

Leo X in 1520. Perugia then became once more an immediate dependency of the Holy See.

Modern Perugia

In 1534, Rodolfo Baglione set fire to the Apostolic palace, and the vice-legate was slain. No sooner had order been established after these events, than a rebellion broke out on account of the tax on salt, which Paul III had increased in 1540. Perugia declared itself a "city of Christ", and confided its keys to the care of a crucifix. On 5 July, however, it was compelled to surrender to the troops of Pierluigi Farnese and lost its freedom. Pope Paul III built a fortress to prevent further revolts by the Perugians, while Pope Julius III restored to them the greater part of their privileges. In the rebellion of 1848, the first act of the Perugians was to demolish the tower of Pope Paul III. In 1859, a provisional Government established, but the Pontifical troops soon took possession of the city.

Finally, in 1860 General de Sonnaz took possession of the town in the name of the King of Sardinia

Perugia Province

Spoleto

Located just a few kilometers from the Valnerina, occupying an impressive hillside position, Spoleto feels very civilized surrounded by a very rural backdrop. Midway between Rome and the late imperial capital Ravenna along the Via Flaminia, Spoleto was one of the few towns able to prosper in the twilight of the empire. Most famous for its famous Festival dei Due Mondi held every summer since 1957, Spoleto is often considered one of Umbria's most graceful hill towns. Apart from the three week long festival of the arts, Spoleto also has a good collection of Roman and medieval attractions that ensure a visit anytime of the year will be enjoyable. The Umbri were the first to settle Spoleto, but it was soon taken over by the Romans who fortified the city walls by building an aqueduct across the gorge, serving as a foundation for the amazing Ponte dell Torri. Ancient churches set in and about Spoleto reflect the town's importance during the early Christian period when it ruled over a large independent duchy. By the 14th century, Spoleto fell under church control, and the Rocca was built at its summit to enforce papal rule.

How to Get to Spoleto By car, Spoleto is on E45 and about a one hour drive from Perugia. From Perugia take the Assisi/Foligno exit and merge onto the SS75 until you exit at Foligno Est exit. Merge onto SS3 and follow signs to Spoleto. There are signs for various parking areas as you enter the town. By train, the main connections are from Rome, Florence, Perugia, and Assisi. The train station is an uphill 15 minute walk into town, so it is best to take a taxi from the station.

Just over Ponte Sanguinario, the gateway into town, is Piazza Garibaldi, where you will find the Church of San Gregorio Maggiore. Originally erected in the 4th century outside the town, it was renovated in the 12th century. Through the gate are the ruins of the Ponte Sanguinario, or Bloody Bridge, which supposedly was named after the Christians martyred in the amphitheater. From Piazza Garibaldi along Via dell'Anfiteatro you will first pass the 2nd century ruins of the Roman amphitheater and then come to Via Cecili and San Nicoli, an imposing deconsecrated Gothic church that now is used for plays and concerts.

If you arrive in Spoleto by bus or car, you are likely to end up at Piazza della Liberta. Across from the tourist office is the Roman theater built in the 1st century AD. It has now been restored to host concerts and ballets during the festival season. The nearby monastery of Sant'Agata, one of the oldest religious buildings in the city is the home of the Museo Archeologico Nazionale. The museum has many important pre-Roman finds along with busts of Julius Caesar, Augustus as well as other important Romans.

Climbing up towards the older part of Spoleto, you will come to Sant'Ansano, a church built on the ruins of a 1st century temple. The church has a mixed history although some of what you see today was completed in the 18th century. Within the church, the 11th century crypt of San Isacco has stayed pretty much the same, and is decorated with frescoes in the Byzantine style. From Sant'Asano Via Arco di Druso you will enter Piazza del Mercato home of the 18th century Fonte di Piazza, a smaller version of Rome's Trevi Fountain.

Close by is Casa Romana, a Roman house dating back to the 1st century. According to legend, the home belonged to Vespasia Polla, the mother of the Emperor Vespasian. The home does display a look at what a noble Roman home would look like in that period, and some rooms have intricate mosaics.

Not far from Piazza Mercato is Spoleto's cathedral. Originally built and consecrated at the end of the 12th century, the cathedral is dedicated to Santa Maria Assunta and sits over the position of two earlier religious buildings. The facade of the church is 12th century Romanesque, that was lightened up by the addition of a Rennaissance loggia, eight rose windows, and a 13th century gold mosaic of Benedictory Christ. The original pavement dates from an earlier church that was destroyed by Frederick I.

Above the entrance is Bernini's bust of Pope Urban VIII who had the rest of the church redecorated in 17th century Baroque. The interior of the church is built on a Latin cross plan, and is divided into three aisles separated by a colonnade. Some of the more important works of art found within the cathedral include the series of rich frescoes of the Life of the Virgin by Florentine Fra Filippo Lippi. Other important works that should be noted are the Cappella del Vescovo Constantino Eroli which was built in 1497 and entirely decorated with frescoes by Pinturicchio, and the frescoes in the chapel alter niche depicting God the Father and Angels, The Madonna and Child, and John the Baptist.

In Piazza Campello sits the 17th century fountain, the Macherone which has a huge face spitting out water from the Roman and medieval aqueduct. The monument on the square dates back to 1910 and was built to honor all of the Spoletines who fought to free Spoleto from the Papal State. La Rocca, a huge fortress sitting just above this monument was built on the orders of Cardinal Albornoz, as his personal headquarters at a time when the church considered Spoleto an outpost and was intent on conquering Umbria.

A short walk from the Ponte dell Torri is the Church of San Pietro. The most impressive aspect of this church is the 12th century sculptures on it's facade that are considered some of the finest Romanesque carvings in Umbria.

Important Festivals

Festival dei Due Mondi, the Festival of Two Worlds runs three weeks from the end of June to mid-July. It has been one of Italy's leading arts festivals with music, theatre, and dance.

Tourist Information Office
Piazza della Liberta 7

Ph 0743 23 89 20/1

8:30am-1:30pm & 4-7pm Monday thru Friday

9:30am-12:30pm Saturday & Sunday

Assisi

The small town of Assisi is one of the Christian world's most important pilgrimage sites as it is home of the Basilica di San Francesco. This small town has been an important place of pilgrimage for over 700 years and today now attracts an estimated 5 million visitors each year. Perched high above the flat valley floor next to Monte Subasio, the cobbled streets of Assisi wind across the hill with spectacular views of the valley below. Like most other towns in the region, Assisi began as an Umbrian settlement in the 7th century BC, was then conquered by the Romans 400 years later. Although the town was Christianized by Saint Rufino, its patron saint in the third century, Assisi will always be known for Saint Francis, a patron saint of Italy who founded the Franciscan monastic order. It is said though, that even without its amazing churches and extraordinary works of art, that it is worth visiting Assisi simply for the sunset. As the sun sets, the entire town is bathed in a warm glow as the sun brings to life the reddish hues of the stone from Monte Subasio that was used in building most of the buildings in town. Assisi has now recovered from the devastating earthquake of 1997 which all but collapsed the Basilica although some minor works of art were forever lost.

How To Get To Assisi - There are hourly trains arriving at the train station in Santa Maria deli Angeli from Foligno and Terontola which is located 5 km from Assisi. Buses run from the train station to Piazza Unita d'Italia in Assisi every 30 minutes. The main bus terminal in Assisi is located in Piazza

Matteotti, above the Duomo which has a full schedule of departures and arrivals to and from many of the local towns. There is one long distance bus that heads to Piazza Adua in Florence and Naples from Piazza San Pietro. You can buy tickets on the bus, or at the Stopini agent at Corso Mazzini 31.

If arriving by car, Assisi now has many car parks just outside the town since parking in the center is impossible. A large underground parking structure can be found at Piazza Matteotti, or in Piazza Unita d'Italia. Other car parks can be found at Porta Nuova and Porta Moiano.

What To See in Assisi - The Basilica di San Francesco ranks second only to St Peter's in Rome as a point of Catholic pilgrimage. The magnificent paintings found within the Basiclica by Giotto have long been considered on of the turning points in

Western art, moving from the Byzantine world of iconic saints and Madonnas, to one with a much more humanist view. The Basilica was built in two tiers, with the Upper Church situated above the Lower Church. Construction of the lower church began 18 months after the death of Saint Francis in 1226 in his honor and was consecrated by the Pope in 1253 although the chapel of Santa Caterina was not completed until 1367.

Lower Church The lower church displays stained-glass windows from Germany, England, and Flanders brought to Assisi during the 13th century. In the center of the lower church above the main alter are four frescoes attributed to Maestro dell Vele, a pupil of Giotto which represent what St Francis described as "the four greatest allegories", including evil, poverty, obedience, and chastity. When you first enter the dark lower church, in the first chapel to the left is a set of frescoes by

Simone Martini depicting scenes from the life of St. Martin. In the transept to the left, Pietro Lorenzetti's Madonna and Child With St. Francis and St. John can be found which sparkles when sunlight strikes it. In the right transept, Cimabue's Madonna Enthroned Among Angels And St. Francis can be found surrounded by paintings of scenes from the childhood of Christ created as well by students of Giotto. Close by is a painting of the crucifixion completed by Giotto himself. Another area of the lower church not to be missed is below the church in the crypt where the stone coffin that holds the body of St. Francis can be found.

Upper Church The upper church was built shortly after the lower one between 1230 and 1253 and has a completely different feeling and look to the darker, more austere lower church. Possibly one of the most famous pieces of art in the world is the 28 part fresco circling the church walls that has been attributed to have been completed by Giotto. Above each image is a corresponding biblical fresco from both the Old and New Testaments. The choir has 105 inlaid stalls that were completed in the 15th century of great detail, most depicting famous Franciscans. The central throne is a papal seat, the only one in the country outside of St. Peter's Basilica in Rome. Behind the throne and in the left transept are frescoes by Cimabue.

Just a short walk from the Basilica along Via Frate Elia you will find the Church of San Pietro which was founded along with the monastery by the Benedictines in the 10th century. The church was consecrated in 1254. San Pietro has now been restored to its previous Romanesque-Gothic state, and although its interior does not boast any important works of art, its simply and high nave are worth a visit.

East of San Pietro you will come to Piazza del Vescovado which was an important square back in the Middle Ages. It houses the Palazzo Vescovile or Bishop's Palace and the Church of Santa Maria Maggiore. The church was thought to have been built in the 10th century, but was rebuilt in 1163 with the Romanesque look it has today.

On the hill above Assisi sits the Rocca Maggiore dates back to Charlemagne who is said to have raised the first walls here after attacking the town. Cardinal Albornoz who arrived in the area in 1367 to assert Papal authority repaired the castle. The views from the top are well worth the trip and you can climb to the top of the polygonal tower.

At the opposite end of Assisi from the Basilica di San Francesco you can find the large Basilica di Santa Chiara. This church is well worth a visit to see the large rose window, flying buttresses, and large piazza out in front that has some amazing views of the local countryside. Inside the church are some frescoes that have yet to be restored, and in the crypt below, Clare's body can be seen in her tomb. In a cabinet nearby are locks of her hair and one of her cloaks. Clare was born into a prominent noble family, but renounced her wealth to follow the example of St. Francis even going as far to set up the convent at San Damiano known as the Poor Clares.

Assisi's 12th century Duomo can be found just east along the narrow streets from Piazza del Comune. The Cathedral di San Ruffino has a typical three tiered facade and Romanesque portal. It is thought that the first church was built on the site to hold the bones of San Ruffino back in 412. San Ruffino was Assisi's first Bishop and was martyred 170 years before construction of the church began. Inside the church is the font that was used to baptize St Francis, St. Clare, and even possibly the emperor Frederick ll.

If you leave Assisi from Porta Nuova, after a 15 minute walk you will come to the Santuary of San Damiano, a Franciscan church that was said to be one of the most important places in the life of St. Francis. It was here that it was said St. Francis heard the voice of God asking him to repair the church spoken through the crucifix which now can be found in the Basilica di Santa Chiara.

At the bottom of the hill, 4km from Assisi you will come to the Basilica di Santa Maria deli Angeli where it is said St. Francis came to live after abandoning all his worldly possessions to live in a small chapel in the woods. St. Francis founded his order of friars here, and even died here in 1226. Although the small chapel, oratory of the Porziuncola still exists today, a grand basilica was built to accommodate it on the spot of pilgrimage by Pope Pius V in the 16th century to honor St. Francis. The great cupola outside along with one of the two bell towers was built by Galeazzo Alessi in 1667. Inside the huge church, along with the old oratory (Capella della Porziuncola) is the Capella del Transito, the old infirmary cell where St. Francis died in October 1226. The chapel even contains the original door.

Basilica di San Franciso is open 6:30am to 6:30pm Monday through Saturdays from Easter through October. The Basilica is open 6:30am to 7:15pm on Sundays and Public Holidays.

Important Festivals
Settimana Santa is celebrated with processions and performances and held during Easter week.

Festa di Calendimaggio is a colorful festival which celebrates spring in medieval fashion. The festivities begin the first Thursday after May 1st.

Festa di San Francesco is the main religious celebration and takes place yearly on October 3 and 4.

Marcia della Pace is Europe's largest peace march. It began in 1961 and attracts thousands who walk the 24 km route between Perugia and Assisi the first week in October.

Assisi Tourist Information

Piazza del Commune 22

8am-2pm & 3pm-6pm Monday through Saturday

Sunday open 9am to 1pm

Ph 075 8138680

Foligno

Foligno is one of Umbria's larger cities that lies in the plain of the river Topino making it one of the few Umbrian towns to be built on flat land. In the past, Foligno was at the crossroads of two important commercial roads, the Via Flaminia and the road from Perugia to Assisi. Unfortunately Foligno was hit by an earthquake in 1997 which did quite a bit of damage to the city, though much of it has now been restored. Foligno is one of Umbria's most important commercial and manufacturing centers so is often overlooked as a tourist destination. It is however a very active city with great shopping, restaurants, and a number of historical sites worth visiting.

How to Arrive in Foligno Foligno lies directly on the Rome/Ancona train line making it easily accessible by train. Buses run from Foligno to Montefalco, Bevagna, Trevi, Spoleto. Assisi and Perugia. The bus station can be found on Viale Mezzetti. Parking is limited in the city center although an underground car park can be found near Porta Romana which is also close to the tourist office.

What to See in Foligno - Piazza della Repubblica is said to be the center of the town and is where you can find the Duomo facing the Palazzo Comunale. The Duomo is of interest as it actually has two facades. The main facade faces Piazza del Duomo, but the more interesting facade can be found on the south side which looks out to Piazza della Republica. The Duomo was started in 1133, added to through 1512, and was restored to it's present Romanesque appearance in the 20th century. The Palazzo Comunale has a Neo-Classical facade and was originally built in the 13th century. The palace was rebuilt several times, retaining only it's original tower which unfortunately was destroyed in the 1997 earthquake. The palace is linked to Palazzo Orfini where it is thought was the home of the painting house of Orfini, one of the earliest of all Italian painting houses.

At the western end of the piazza is the Palazzo Trinci which has been altered many times throughout the years and now is home of the Pinacoteca Communale and the Museo Archeologico. The interior of Palazzo Trinci dates back to the period of Ugolino III Trinci who ruled from 1386 until 1415. You can view many paintings and frescoes within Palazzo Trinc, including important works by Ottaviano Nelli, Niccolo Alunno, and Pier Antonio Mezzastris.

If you follow Via Gramsci from piazza you will pass by many of the Folignati palaces including the 16th century Palazzo Deli which is considered one of the most attractive and features a medieval tower that once was part of Palazzo Trinci.

The Church of Santa Maria Infraportas at the end of Via Gramsci is one of Foligno's oldest churches and has unusual 12th century windows and portico as well as frescoes by Mezzastris and others.

Although other churches in Foligno are also contain some important artwork, one of the more important ones is the Church of San Niccolo on Via della Scuola di Arti e Mestieri which was rebuilt in the 14th century by Olivetan monks, then rebuilt in the 18th century. This church houses works by Foligno's own Niccolo di Liberatore, known as Alunno including the Polyptych of the Nativity which is considered one of his best works.

If one heads east from Foligno on road #77 for 2 kilometers you will come to a road that leads up to the Abazia di Sassovivo, the 11th century Benedictine abbey with a 13th century Romanesque cloister. The cloister features 128 columns that support 58 arches that are decorated with marbles and mosaics.

Important Festivals

The Giostra della Quintana which takes place on the weekend closest to June 14-15 is a 17th century custom that involves knights from 10 districts jousting, historical foods, games, and parades.

I Primi D'Italia

I Primi d'Italia is a food festival that takes place the end of September in locations across the city centre in a four day event. The event highlights the world of the first courses with options from many regions across Italy.

Market Days

Markets in Foligno take place on Tuesday and Saturday on Via Nazario Sauro.

Foligno Tourist Office

Corso Cavour 126

Phone 0742-354459

Montefalco

Often nicknamed the balcony of Umbria, Montefalco is famous for its Sagrantino wine and its position high in the hills which allows one views over to Perugia, Assisi and even Spoleto. Although Montefalco today still retains some elements of its Roman origin, the atmosphere of this charming small wine town is very medieval. Although primarily known today for its textiles and wine, this tiny town also produced six saints over the centuries which is reflected in its impressive frescoed churches.

Until 1240 Montefalco was known as Coccorone when Frederick II destroyed it and rebuilt it as a Ghibelline town and ten named it after his imperial eagle. Montefalco later became part of the domain of the Trinci family, and later was overseen by the church.

How to Arrive in Montefalco There are two trains daily to and from Foligno and SSIT buses to Montefalco from Bastardo, Bevagna, and Perugia once a day, and from Foligno several times each day. If driving, there is a large car park just outside the main walls of town.

What To See In Montefalco The main access into town is the impressive 14th century Porta Sant'Agostino which has a tower on top. From here one heads up Via Umberto and then Corso Mameli into the main square Piazza del Commune. Along the way to the main piazza you'll pass the Church of Sant'Agostino which originates from the late 13th century. The exterior facade is decorated with slender columns and a lovely rose window while the interior houses a number of beautiful frescoes.

The central piazza to which the rest of the streets spoke out from is home to Palazzo Comunale, the former Church of Sa Filippo Neri which is now a theater, and the Oratorio di Santa Maria. Just north from the main piazza along Via Ringhiera Umbra is perhaps Montefalco's most important monument, the deconsecrated 14th century Church of San Francesco. The church houses the frescoes painted by Benozzo Gozzoli. The attached monastery houses the Museo Communale and both buildings display artwork salvaged from other local churches.

From Piazza del Comune, if you take the stairs leading south you'll come across the Church of San Bartolomeo as well as a gate with the same name. Walking westward away from the old walls you will reach the convent and Church of Santa Chiara, both deicated to Chiara di Damiano of Montefalco (1268-1308).

One shouldn't visit Montefalco without tasting some of the towns wonderful wines, particularly its most famous Sagrantino variety. Go to the information office at Piazza del Comune 17 for maps to local wineries, and information on wine tasting. Many wineries offer free tastings, some charge a small fee, while others, particularly the smaller vintners request that reservations be made before your arrival. Tours of some wineries are offered but generally reservations are required ahead of time for those.

Important Festivals

Fuga del Bove is an ox race that takes place every year in Montefalco. It is a bloodless recalling of a historical game written up in the ancient city chronicles. The bull of each quarter, properly trained during the year, competes against the rivals through an uneven way. This race takes place at the end of the month and is proceeded by weeks of festivities.

Festa dell'Uva, or grape festival takes place at the end of September.

Market Day
Monday is market day in Montefalco at largo Santa Chiara and largo Buozzi.

Tourist Office Piazza Comune 17,
Phone 0742-378490

Trevi

Trevi is a small picturesque town perched high on a hillside surrounded by olives trees as far as one can see. Most of the town is densely built in a spiral fashion around the hilltop with many buildings predating the 18th century. From town one can see one of the best views in Umbria, over 50 km to the west and on clear days as far away as Perugia to the north and even Monte Amiata in southern Tuscany. Trevi is well known across Italy for the high quality of its olive oil and holds a wonderful festival every fall in celebration of the olive oil harvest.

How to Reach Trevi- Arriving in Trevi is been done by car although there are daily buses arriving from Foligno several times a day. Arrival by train is possible from Spello, Assisi, and Perugia, but the train station is several kilometers from the center of town and you must take a bus from the train station to Trevi. If you are driving, there is a large parking lot around Piazza Garibaldi just east of the walls.

What to See Trevi was a theater town back in Roman times and the Teatro Clitunno remains one of the town's most important gathering places. Remnants of the rings of Mura Romana (Roman Wall) and Mura Medieval (Medieval Wall) still can be found encircling the town. The Museo della Civilta dell'Ulivo, or Olive Oil Museum is well worth a visit if you are in the area and can be found in an ex-convent on Lago Don Bosco #14. Although there are a couple of other museums housed in the same building, the olive oil museum is the highlight.

The town's main square Piazza Mazzini is home to the Palazzo Comunale, which was built in the 14th century. Later in the 15th century the large portico was added. From this piazza you can take Via San Francrsco and pass the Palazzo Valenti before coming to the very large Church of San Fransesco. This church along with the adjacent Raccolta d"Arte di San Fransesco is the town's most important artistic attraction and the church is in fact not used for worship anymore. The museum houses a few Roman artifacts, but mostly a good number of Umbrian paintings from the late Middle Ages to the 17th century. The most important painting was once part of an altar, and it is by Lo Spagna. There is also a very interesting group of "ex-votos" (paintings to thank God for saving a person from a sickness or an accident) painted by ordinary people, not famous artists, of the 16th - century to the 18th-century on display.

Also in the center of town on Via della Rocca one comes upon Cattedrale di Sant'Emiliano, or Trevi's Duomo, dedicated to a local saint. The duomo was built in the 12th century and renovated and enlarged in the 15th century. Saint Emiliano who served as the bishop of Trevi in the 4th century is honored every January 27th with a procession of the illuminata.

One kilometer south of Trevi stands the Chiesa della Modonna delle Lacrime where in 1485 it is claimed that the painting of the virgin in a shrine cried tears of blood. To get to the church leave town by Porta del Cieco and head downhill through the olive groves.

From Piazza Garibaldi, outside the gate to the centro storico, take Via Ciuffelli to the 14th century Capuchin monastery and Church of San Martino. Over the door hangs a lunette by Tiberio d'Assisi who also has the painting St Martin and The Beggar inside.

Eight kilometers south of Trevi you can see the Fonti di Clitunno, which is a well-known spot where several springs flow out from the rocks into large clear pools that attract ducks in a park-like setting with lush landscaping. About 500 meters north of the springs one can still find Tempietto del Clitunno on the SS3. It was belieed to be a pagan temple that was later converted to Christian use and thought to have originated in the 7th or 8th century.

Information Office

Piazza Mazzini 5

Phone 0742 781 150

Passignano sul Trasimeno

Passignano is the busiest resort town situated around Lago di Trasimeno. More than a thousand years of art and architecture can be found in this lakeside holiday resort which also offers all kinds of water-sports, tennis, horse-riding, and trekking. The town sits high on its own promontory midway between Cortona and Perugia.

How to Arrive Passignano sul Trasimeno can be easily reached by car, train or bus. By car From Florence along the A1: Exit at Valdichiana, take the Perugia Bettolle highway and exit at Passignano sul Trasimeno. By car from Rome along the E45 Terni-Cesena highway: at Ponte San Giovanni take the Perugia Bettolle highway. Exit at Passignano sul Trasimeno. If arriving by train, you can either take the Ancona-Foligno-Terontola or the Milan-Florence-Rome lines and exit at Terentola. From there you must take either a us or car to Passignano. There are many buses arriving from Perugia that arrive at the lake daily.

What To See In Passignano The oldest historical center of Passignano sul Trasimeno is still today encircled by the middle age walls which reflect the development the area underwent during the Roman Empire. Passignano evolved from a small agricultural village to a castle, which, after the

Lordship of Uguccione II in the 917, was constantly aimed at by Arezzo, Perugia and Florence. Although visitors cannot tour the castle, it is worth a walk up to see the wonderful views across the lake and surrounding countryseide. Unfortunately, not very many historical buildings are left in the town due to the destructions caused by the II the world war bombings. All that remains is in fact the Church of S. Rocco , from the 15th century, and S. Bernardino, erected only a few years later. Near the cemetery, the Pieve di San Cristofo which dates back to the 11th century can be found. It contains restored frescoes that date back to the 1300's. Just a kilometer or two away from the town the elegant Renaissance Church of Modonna dell'Olivio can be found with it's high altar and frescoes attributed to Bartolomeo Caporali.

From Passignano, the Isola Maggiore (Greater Island), on Trasimeno Lake, can be reached in less than 20 minutes by ferry. There, one can visit the Romanesque Church of S. Salvatore of the XII century, that of S. Michele Archangel of the XIV century and the Villa Isabella of Marquises Guglielmi.

For those who love to hike, the surrounding hills around Passignano offer such sites to see as the ruins of the Roman Villa of Quarantaia, or walk to the ancient Fortress of Monteruffiano. Passignano is the head office of the Trasimeno Park Organization.

Important Festivals

The famous Palio delle Barche, traditional boat race, can be viewed on the third Sunday of July. At this time young people of Passignano dress up in medieval costumes and carry their boats on their shoulders in a procession through town and down to the lake where they launch the boats for the race. There is also a fish festival where you can eat seafood cooked in the largest frying-pan in the world, measuring 4,30 meters in Diameter.

Tourist Office Can Be Found @ Castiglione del Lago
Piazza Mazzini, 10
Tel. 075/9652484 Fax. 075/9652763

Spello

Sitting up on a hillside in the shadow of Monte Subasio between Assisi and Foligno, the pink stoned Spello is a perfect example of one of Umbria's medieval small towns. Spello was settled under the Umbri, but grew in size under the Romans in the 1st century BC when it was known as Hispellum. Among it's Umbrian neighbors, Spello is one which preserves the major number of monuments testifying to the Roman era. Most obvious are the town walls, the ruins of the theater and the amphitheater seen just outside of town, the thermal baths, and the splendid town portals Porta Consolare, Porta Urbica and Porta Venere dating back to the Augustean era. Spello also boasts one of Umbria's major art attractions, the outstanding frescoes by Pinturicchio in the church of Santa Maria Maggiore.

How to Get to Spello Regular trains run from Foligno and Perugia and there are up to nine buses that stop in Spello on the Assisi Foligno run. A car park is located immediately after Sant'Andrea and there is a second one off Via Cimitero by Porta Montanara.

What to See in Spello Santa Maria Maggiore is thought to be built over an ancient temple dedicated to Juno and Vesta. The façade has a Romanesque portal and a 13th century bell tower, while the pilasters next to the apse have frescoes by Perugino (1512). The most striking feature is however a very fine chapel (Cappella Bella) frescoed by Pinturicchio. The Umbrian artist was called to paint these frescoes in 1500 by Troilo Baglioni. The fresco cycle include the Annunciation, the Nativity and the Dispute with the Doctors, plus four Sibyls in the vault.

The Palazzo dei Canonici, annexed to the church, houses the Town's Art Gallery, The Pinacoteca Civica. One of the finest pieces inside are a wooden statue the Madonna and Child, an Umbrian work dating back to the end of the 12th century. Also shown is a statue of the crucified Christ.

The Palazzo Comunale Vecchio, or "Old Town Hall", which contains the Library and Town Archive, was built in 1270 and then enlarged after the end of the Baglioni seigniory, in 1567-1575. It too has some frescoed halls, with one attributed to the Zuccari brothers. It is faced by a 16th century fountain.

Along Via Garibaldi you will come across Palazzo Cruciali, built in the early 17th century, the seat of the town council, and then San Lorenzo from the 12th century. San Bernardino da Siena began his preaching season in this church in 1438.

Palazzo Baglioni, erected as a fortificated mansion around 1359. The Governor's Hall has frescoes from the 16th century.

Sant'Andrea lies a short distance uphill from the Pinacoteca and boasts a simple 13th century facade. The interior, on a single nave, has 14th century frescoes. There's also a panel by Pinturicchio, named Madonna and Child with saints.

Along nearby Via Torri di Properzio one comes across Porta Venere, a Roman gateway flanked by two towers and one of the best remnants of Roman Spello. The twin towers flanking the gate might be either Roman or medieval.

Porta dell'Arce is one of the oldest entrances to Spello and is a great example of how the Romans integrated their buildings into their fortifications. Close by, one can see across to Assisi's Santa Maria deli Angeli from the Belvedere.

From the belvedere, you can descend down to San Claudio, an elegant example of Romanesque architecture with a rose window on the asymmetrical façade. The church itself dates back to the 12th century, while the interior has 14th century votive frescoes from the Umbrian school. San Claudio is said to have been built on the remains of a Paleo-Christian cemetery.

In the plain, near San Claudio, are the remains of a semi-excavated Roman Amphitheatre which was built below the medieval town.

Important Festivals

The Infiorata includes a whole night of work for the Corpus Domini feast when the streets are "painted" in artworks with flower petals.

Spello Tourist Office

Piazza Matteotti 3

Ph 0742/301/009

Gualdo Tadino

Just east of Gubbio, Gualdo Tadino is another Umbrian hill town that occupies the site of ancient Tadinum, a Roman staging post on the Via Flaminia. The town is of both Umbrian and Roman origins, and has endured a tormented history until the 12th century when it was resettled on it's present site. Today the town which sprawls across the lower slopes of the Apennines mountains is a quiet place best known for it's ceramics. Gualdo suffered substantially in the 1997 earthquake and has almost been completely restored since then.

How to Get to Gualdo Tadino Gualdo is situated in northeastern Umbria and can be reached by train, or by bus from Gubbio or Foligno. Gualdo Tadino has a railway station on the line from Ancona to Foligno, with some trains continuing through to Rome. The journey time to Ancona is typically one hour and 45 minutes, and to Foligno 40 minutes.

What to See in Gualdo Tadino Gualdo Tadino, famous for its ceramics industry and art, lays on Sant'Angelo hill dominated by the castel "Rocca Flea". Although not considered a historical landmark, the historic town center has some interesting civic and religious buildings.

The Duomo, also known as San Benedetto, is located in the central Piazza Martiri della Liberta and has a facade quite similar to Todi's Duomo. The facade dates back to the 13th century, and had to be carefully restored after the earthquake. The interior was completely rebuilt in the 19th century and hosts some beautiful 20th century frescoes. Outside the church to the left is an attractive Renaissance fountain.

Opposite the cathedral sits the Palazzo Comunale, with origins from the 18th century along with the Palazzo del Podesta.

TheChurch of San Francesco has been deconsecrated and is now used to house temporary exhibitions and features frescoes on the Life of St. Julian by the school of Ottaviano Nelli.

At the top of the hill the Rocca Flea can be found, a fortress whose origins date back to the 10th century when the construction began on the former site of a church. Today the fortress has over 40 rooms and reflect the influence of Frederick II who made improvements to the castle during the 13th century. The Rocca houses a Pinacoteca, or art gallery, a ceramics gallery, and a collection of archeological finds.

Gualdo Tadino Tourist Office

Via Calai 39

ph 075/912/172

Perugia

Perugia is the largest city in Umbria, and is the capital of the province of Perugia. The historic center of the city has a medieval feel to it but is actually based on Etruscan plans. The city symbol is the griffin, which can be seen in the form of plaques and statues on buildings around the city. Perugia today has a cosmopolitan feel to it compared to other cities in the region and is famous for it's world class jazz festival, it's University for Foreigners, and it's chocolates and pastries.

How to Get to Perugia The best approach to the city is by train. Perugia's main train station is named "Stazione Fontivegge," and is located on Piazza Vittorio Veneto, a few kilometres west of the city centre, but buses are frequent from the station to Piazza d'Italia, the heart of old town. Another option of travel is by bus. Intercity buses from surrounding areas in Umbria are both frequent and inexpensive. If traveling by car from the south, exit the A1 at the Orte and follow the signs for Terni. Once there, take the SS3bis/E45 for Perugia. From the north, exit the A1 at Valdichiana and take SS75 for Perugia.

Founded by the Etruscans in 5th century BC, Perugia soon fell to Roman conquer in 309 BC. Almost immediately after, the city was caught between the power struggles of two Roman rulers, and was burned and destroyed in 140 BC. The city was slowly rebuilt during the Middle Ages during which time the city was incorporated in the Papal States. The city remained under papal control for almost three centuries, gaining its independence when the troops of Victor Emmanuel II Of Savoy (1820-1878) conquered the city and unified the entire Italian peninsula. Perugia's hilltop position has enabled the city to be on of the best-preserved hill towns of its size, and few other places in Italy better exemplify the medieval self-contained city state that helped shape the course of Italian history.

What to See in Perugia - Perugia occupies an important position on top of a series of hills near the Tiber River which helps explain how the city has remained almost completely intact. Most of the most important sites to see in Perugia are within it's historical center and can be reached by walking.

The Palazzo Dei Priori is partly situated in the main square on the northern end of Corso Vannucci, the street named after the most important Perugian painter of the Renaissance, Pietro Vannucci. Its construction began in 1293 and was completed in 1442. It is often cited as Italy's most impressive civic place and houses four separate buildings hidden in its grounds; the Sala dei Notari, Sala del Collegio della Mercanzia, Collegio del Cambio and the Galleria Nazionale dell'Umbria.

The Sala dei Notari is one of the oldest parts of the palazzo, dating back to the early 13th century. Before it was used as a medieval lawyer's meeting hall, it was used as a meeting place for townspeople in time of crisis and decision.

The Sala del Collegio della Mercanzia, a room of carved wood reveals intricate wooden paneling that is considered as one of the finest examples of 15th century wooden work throughout Italy. It was the original meeting room for merchants, especially fabric traders.

The Collegio del Cambio is located on the ground floor of the palazzo and served as the meeting hall and chapel of the guild of bankers and moneychangers. Its walls are covered with frescoes done by Pietro Vannucci, better know as Perugino, which are reckoned to be one the best-preserved Renaissance schemes in the country.

The National Gallery of Umbria is located on the fourth floor of the Palazzo dei Priori and was established in 1863 and is the region's main repository of Umbrian art.

Situated in the Piazza Forebraccio is the Acro di Augusto (Arch of Augustus). Dating from 3rd century BC, this arch was the main entrance to the Etruscan and Roman acropolis. Located in the same square is the Universita per Stranieri (University for Foreigners).

Also called the Cathedral of San Lorenzo, the Duomo, is most famous for being the home of the wedding ring of the Virgin Mary. It is located in the main square and was built between the years 1437 to 1587. Outside the Duomo is the Fontana Maggiore, which was built prior to the Duomo in 1287, and is adorned with zodiac figures and symbols of the seven arts.

Important Festivals
Every July Perugia plays host to Italy's foremost

Jazz festival, Umbria Jazz, whose stars have included Miles Davis, Stan Getz and Wynton Marsalis. During this two-week festival hundreds of concerts all over the town of Perugia offer a musical variety rarely seen and heard elsewhere.

In mid- to late September, Perugia hosts Sagra Musicale Umbra, one of the oldest music festivals in Europe that features world reknown conductors and musicians.

In the month of October, Perugia welcomes the weeklong festival entitled Eurochocolate. Stalls and vendors line the streets of Perugia, offering the public their best creation. Films are show, workshops and competitions are held, and exhibitions are opened; all in the spirit of chocolate. Every year the event increases in intensity and participation from the public.

In November in Pian Massiano is the Fiera dei Morti, the oldest fair in Italy.

Market Days

Saturday mornings in the Pian di Massiano.

Daily markets near the Kennedy escalator off Piazza Matteoti.

Thursday market at Ponte San Giovanne (Perugia)

Perugia Tourist Office

Piazza Matteotti 18, 06100 Perugia

Open 8-12am and 4pm until sunset.

Phone- 075 573 6458

Fax: 075 573 9386

The main tourist office is at Piazza IV Novembre under the arches near the flight of steps and behind the fountain.

Gubbio

Gubbio is one of northern Umbria's most stunning stone hill towns, and stands at the foot of Mount Ingino. It is difficult not to be awed by the stark beauty of this medieval town as you approach by car and see it's grey limestone buildings built along it's steep streets that wind up the base of the mountain. Founded by the Umbri, the town holds the famous Eugubine Tablets, which are seven bronze slabs that have managed to survive from the ancient city of Iguvium which are presently held in the Museo Civico. These tablets were engraved in the 2nd century with text in local languages describing sacred rites and sites.

How to Reach Gubbio By car, the most likely route to Gubbio is on the SS298 road from Perugia. There are ASP frequent buses running from Citta di Castello and Perugia to Gubbio, as well as once daily direct buses from both Florence and Rome. The closest train station is Fossato di Vico, which is

19 kilometers south on the Rome/Foligno line. From Fossato di Vico you may catch a bus to Gubbio upon arrival. Parking can be found at Piazza Quaranta Marti every day except Tuesday, or off of Viale di Teatro Romano.

What to See in Gubbio After the Umbrians founded Gubbio it was later held by the Romans who began to build outwards allowing the town to spread onto the surrounding plain. After repeated raids by Barbarians however, the people of Gubbio returned to the slopes along the mountain so they could better protect themselves. Gubbio was once a walled city that included the massive Palazzo dei Consoli in the Middle Ages, but later passed on to Montefeltro of Urbino, and in 1624 Gubbio came under papal rule.

As you approach Gubbio, the first Roman monument you will see are the ruins of the Roman

Theater which dates as far back as the 1st century. In it's day, this theater could hold 6,000 spectators.

Chiesa San Francesco is considered Gubbio's finest church and sits in Piazza Quaranta Martiri, found at the lowest point of Gubbio. This piazza was named after forty local residents who were killed by the Germans during the war in retaliation for partisan attacks in the surrounding hills. San Francesco dates back to the mid 1200's and construction continued through the end of that century although the exterior facade has never been completed. Within the church are a cycle of fading, yet still impressive frescoes painted by Ottaviano Nelli around 1410. A small chapel in the sacristy is said to be the room where St. Francis slept on his visits to Gubbio.

Across from San Francesco is Antico Ospedale, an old hospital that dates back to the 14th century. A long portico was added in front of the building in the 17th century by wool merchants who stetted out their ear under the portico to prevent it being dried too quickly by the sun.

Just behind the loggia on Via dell Repubblica you find the Chiesa di San Giovanni Battista which has been restored to its thirteenth century state. The church has a Gothic facade with an oddly shaped Romanesque bell tower.

In Piazza Grande, you can find one of the most outstanding sites in Gubbio, which is the austere 14th century Palazzo dei Consoli which has a 98 meter campanile. It is thought to have been designed by Matteo Gattapone who was also responsible for Spoleto's Ponte dell Torri. This palace took a couple hundred years to build and required leveling of vast tracts of the town.

The lesser Palazzo Pretorio opposite was built along the same plan. Behind a small square facade is a small hole on the top right where criminals were hung.

The Museo Civico is also based here and includes a small archeological collection, not terribly remarkable apart from the Eugubine Tablets, Umbria's most important archeological find. Admission to this museum also gives you admission into the five roomed Pinacoteca at the top of the palace, which houses some works by the Gubbian School, one of central Italy's earliest, including a collection of oversized 14th century furniture.

To the north of Piazza Grande is the unimposing 13th century Duomo, which is only partly redeemed by a few frescoes, 12th century stained glass, and some attractive arches carved to appear as hands in prayer.

The plain faced Gothic cathedral is entirely overshadowed by the Palazzo Ducale in Via Federico da Montefeltro. It was built over an earlier Lombard palace by the Dukes of Montefeltro as a smaller version of their more famous palace in Urbino. Although the courtyard is quite pretty, the interior has been stripped of most of it's art work and furnishings.

From Piazza Grande, take Via XX Setembre to the quarter of Sant'Andrea to find the Porta Romana. This medieval town gate with it's high tower houses a collection of majolica pottery and other pieces such as weaponry and maps.

On the hill above the town stands the Basilica of Sant'Ubaldo where you can enjoy some lovely views of the town and surrounding countryside.

You can rearch the basilica by walking a steep track that runs behind the Duomo, or by taking the funicular from Porta Romana on the eastern side of town.

Important Festivals

Corsa dei Ceri This candle race is to Umbria what the Palio is to Siena and takes place every year on May 15th and finishes at the hilltop basilica of Sant'Ubaldo.

Gubbio Tourist Office Piazza Odersi 6 (Off of Corso Garibaldi)

Ph 075 9220790

email info@iat.gubbio.pg.it

Perugia Tourism
Tourist Attractions

These are organized roughly in order of preference, though of course this is just my opinion. Note that some of the best things are free. There's also lots of other stuff to do -ask people who have been here a while. These are sort of the basic, inexpensive, touristy things, though don't leave them all for your last days here.

Le Scalette > The long steps on the side of the cathedral have likely hosted the young (or at least tired) of the city for centuries. This is my favorite place to sit and relax. An old Perugian leaned over one day and told me, "*Ste scale sono la spiaggia di*

Perugia, e la gente, le onde," which means "These steps are the beach of Perugia, and the people in the piazza, the waves." It's free, you always meet people, and you can people-watch to your heart's content. You might even get a harangue from Mauro the Prophet, the crazy guy in a jogging suit who occasionally preaches at the top of his lungs. At some point turn around and look at the Duomo, noting that the pink and white façade was never finished. Close your eyes and imagine masons six hundred years ago putting down their tools and saying "*la finiamo domani*!"

Want to learn some of Perugia's cool history? Check out the new book *Home Street Home: Perugia's History Told Through Its Streets*.

The panorama walk > You're up on a hill surrounded, at least on three sides, by beautiful valleys. Enjoy these vistas. Start with the one behind the Provincial building on Piazza Italia, in the Giardini Carducci. It's populated mostly by cooing couples at night, when the lights of the city below sparkle. If you go to the far corner of the gardens and cross the street, there's an overlook and a drawing explaining the sights (which mountains are which, etc.) next head down Via Baglioni (Corso Vannucci's parallel) to where it widens to become Piazza Matteotti.

Now head out to the panorama on top of the Mercato Coperto: at Piazza Matteotti 18A, go through a little arch/tunnel, go around the stands selling clothing, and to the terrace. Look out across the valley towards the city on the far side of the valley halfway up the mountain, Assisi. The mountain above Assisi is Monte subasio Perugians say "*Quando il subasio ha il cappello, esci con l'ombrello.*" The two spires to your right are San Domenico (the nearest) and San Pietro. When it's foggy the valley will fill up so that Assisi looks like a port on the far side of a big lake.

From here, go back to Piazza IV Novembre. Go around the right side of the Duomo and up Via del Sole, the only road that ascends. Go up and bear left when it becomes Via delle Prome. At the end, you'll find the best picture in Perugia. Off to your right you can see the medieval walls and the Monteluce neighborhood. The area where you are now, known as Porta Sole, is the highest, publicly accessible point in Perugia. You are standing on the remains of a fourteenth century addition to the city's fortifications. As you descend the steps you can catch a glimpse of the supporting arches (and the green door).

After you take a picture, go down the steps to your left. The area behind the green door is the vineyard we take care of with Dave and David. At the bottom of the steps, continue down along the wall to Piazza Fortebraccio. Noting the Etruscan Arch on your left, cross the piazza to Palazzo Gallenga, and go up the stairs in front of you as you enter and act like you know where you're going. At the very top you'll find a great terrace that will give you a perfect view of the twelfth century aqueduct (via dell'acquedotto, now a cool footbridge) that occasionally in its eight hundred year existence brought water to the Fontana Maggiore. Go back down and snaffle an ice cream at the nearby *gelateria*, Augusta Perusia, at Via Pinturicchio 2 and eat it sitting on the overlook off to the right of the Etruscan Arch.

San Francesco and Sant'Angelo > Two other great places to relax and catch some sun. The first is the lawn outside of San Francesco: follow Via dei Priori down until near the end, bearing right as it becomes Via San Francesco. It's one of the only places in the center level enough for a good football match. Sant'Angelo is closer to the University for Foreigners. Follow Corso Garibaldi up all the way to the massive gate, Porta Sant'Angelo, and go up the stairs to your right to the Chiesa di Sant'Angelo. The nearby thirteenth century defensive tower is also a visitable attraction, offering a small museum about the city walls and panoramic views. Open 11-13:30 and 15-17:00 (daily except Tuesdays). The €2.50 entry ticket includes access to the Pozzo Etrusco and San Severo.

Perugina Chocolate Factory > Now owned by Nestlè, the iconic chocolate factory has been around for a long time. It's a bit outside the city, about half an hour. Get there with a bus from Piazza Partigiani; tell the bus driver you want to get off at the Perugina. Open Mo-Fr 9-13:00, 14-17:30. You have to make an appointment for the tour. Call the free toll 800.800.907. And yes, they do give you free *baci* (kisses), which make Hershey's kisses taste like spinach-so be sure to try one. They all have little love sayings in four or five languages inside the wrapper. You can also go to their store at 101 Corso Vannucci, near Piazza Italia, if all you want to do is buy great chocolate. Cost of the factory tour and tasting:7 €

The Umbrian National Gallery > I finally went there for the first time with my friend Laura after three years of living here. It's in the Palazzo dei Priori and open 8:30¬19:30, and Saturdays a bit longer. There is a lot of medieval and renaissance art as well as work by Perugia's hometown boy, Perugino. As Francesco, one of my Italian friends, tells me, Perugino's real name was Pietro Vannucci, hence the street. The gallery features paintings on canvas, wood and masonry, sculptures in wood and stone, jewelry and textiles.

More info at www.gallerianazionaleuMbria.it. Audio guides available.

Academy of Fine Arts of Perugia > We often take a dim view of Italy's artistic heritage—mainly because most museums simply have too much set out, with little explanation. The Accademia di Belle Arti di Perugia is a refreshing exception to this. From Corso Vannucci, walk all the way down Via dei Priori and when you see steps in front of you descending to a large city gate, bear off to the right in Via San Francesco. Walk fifty meters and you'll see the church: go through the door between the big church on the right and the chapel on the left. Walk down the ramp and keep going straight. With a ticket (€5, €3 reduced), and you can then go into the Plaster Casts Gallery and the Pinacoteca.

"Plaster casts? Boorrrring!" you would think. But no, it's pretty cool: there are casts (some centuries old) of a lot of famous statues that you may not be able to go see: the *Dying Gaul*, two of Michangelo's *Prisoners*, the *Laocoön and His Sons* (the sea serpernt has just grabbed them outside Troy's gates!), even the reconstructed façade of a Roman temple. The Pinacoteca is like the Plaster Casts Gallery: not too much. There are maybe fifty frames on the walls, so it's a great panorama of four centuries of work, but not overwhelming. Open Sa 14:30-17, and Su 10:30-13 & 14:30-17.

Museum of the City Walls > Explore this neat little museum that is located inside the Porta Sant'Angelo at the end of Corso Garibaldi. It's housed in the Sant'Angelo tower, the largest remaining item of the defensive structures that once served to keep nasties out of the city. The museum display explains the development of Perugia's three rings of city walls, constructed variously during the Etruscan, Medieval and

Renaissance epochs. The summit has arguably the best 360-degree view of the city. You also get the tower well-fresco combo-card so you can see that large Etruscan hole with water at the bottom and Raffaelo's chapel up on Porta Sole. Open 11-13:30 & 15-17:00, daily except Tuesdays.

The Pauline Fortress > You don't need the museum ticket to see the fortress. This area used to be Perugia's swanky neighborhood, with the houses of all its rebellious nobles. Then came the salt war with the Pope and the entire area was razed. An enormous fortress, the Rocca Paolina, was built to keep Perugia under the papal thumb. It was so well fortified that, according to Zach's shady former landlord, the Pope always fled there if there was trouble in Rome. Centuries of being papal lackeys made the populace tear down the rocca after unification in 1848. They got a little carried away and used explosives and a piece of the rocca fell on passers-by in Via Mazzini (near the fountain), but the basement still is there. Go down the escalators on the right side of the big building on Piazza Italia, and imagine being imprisoned here by the vicar of the Prince of Peace. At the bottom of the first escalator and around to the left are several maps of the "before and after" of Perugia's biggest makeover.

Palazzo dei Priori > At the other end of Corso Vannucci is the Palazzo dei Priori, the town hall of Perugia. Go up the round set of steps on the side of the Palazzo nearest the fountain and check out (for free) the hall of the notaries. It was here that the Perugian nobles met in splendor to decide how to squeeze even more money out of the peasants. The hall is often used for special occasions and concerts.

P.O.S.T > Nope, no long lines to lick a stamp here. This is Perugia's Science Museum, right next to the *informagiovani* office. It's pretty sweet, and worth the couple euros to get in. It's open Sat 15:30-19, Sun and holidays 15:30-19.

The Etruscan Well > This well is thirty-six metres deep and was dug by the Etruscans; it remained the principal source of water for the city well into the Middle Ages. The covered top of the well is in the middle of Piazza Piccinino, but you'll have to go down a little alleyway from just before the piazza to actually look into it (look for signs). We heard that after the Americans bombed the water lines to the city at the end of the Second World War, Perugians used the 2,300-year-old well to keep from dying of thirst. If you're not having a grand Museum day, your ticket for the Etruscan well also includes entry to San Severo (see Raphael's fresco below) and the Sant'Angelo tower (see Museum of the City Walls above) at the top end of Corso Garribaldi. It's not a bad value for €2.50. Hours 10:30-13:30 & 14:30-17:00, closed Tuesdays.

Raphael's Fresco > Painting his first fresco in an obscure church didn't adversely affect the career of Raphael. Dating back to 1505, his "*trinità*" can be found in the chapel adjacent to the Chiesa di San Severo above Piazza Piccinino. There's also a "Mary with Jesus" in terracotta for all you "Madonna col bambino" fans. 10:30-13.30 & 14:30-17:00 every day except Tuesday. Tuesday is apparently not a good Museum day.

Hostels and Hotels in Perugia

If Perugia is your vacation destination, there are hotels, hostels, and bed and breakfast's to fit all budgets.

For students traveling abroad, the hardest part of planning a trip is figuring out where you'll be sleeping. Many hostels are cheap, but located miles from big-city main attractions. For families and parents visiting, there are quaint hotels with great prices.

So have no fear! Perugia has plenty of options in close proximity to the city's exciting nightlife.

*Note that this page is not advertising. These listings are based on our knowledge and reviews from several students ad travellers in Perugia

Perugia Hostels

Youth Hostel of Perugia

The Youth Hostel of Perugia is located right downtown, near the main square of the city. This hostel is a main choice for young travelers, with its ideal location and price of 17 euros a night. Your 17 euros insures your bed- fit with linens, and gives you access to the kitchen, TV room, library, and showers.

(When traveling as a student, always ask about student discounts with your school I.D.)

Little Italy Hostel
Little Italy Hostel is a beautiful. modern (luxury I would say) hostel right downtown Perugia. Affordable price, around 18 euros per night and also have group options. The hostel was an ancient eleventh century church, now you can still see typical architectural elements and original frescos. Free wifi, sheets and blankets, welcome gift, TV, Chill-out area, bar, security lockers. You are provided with electronic key and have access 24h/24h. It's int he historical center and close to all the attractions and bars….if you think their bar is not enough. They also host parties with DJs and locals.

Spagnoli Hostel

Hostel Spagnoli is a great option for students and family who are staying in Perugia on a limited budget. Located in the outskirts of Perugia, it is a short minimetro ride to the center. Children and teens (5 years to 18 years old) have discounted fees. This youth hostel has free wifi, free breakfast every morning, and bed linens included. With prices starting at 18 euros, this bed&breakfast style hostel is a steal!

Some Perugia Hotels (in the historical center)

Hotel Anna

Hotel Anna is a generously priced hotel located in the middle of Perugia's historial city center. Free breakfast is served every morning by the owners of this quaint Perugian hotel, and all the rooms include a bathroom, TV, and telephone. For it's spectacular location, on Via dei Priori, it is a sensible choice for weekend visitors. Room prices per night start at 35 euros!

Hotel Morlacchi
Hotel Morlacchi has a charming atmosphere and is the perfect stay for families and parents visting Perugia. Located at Via Leopoldo Tiberi, it is only a few minutes from the historical center. The prices range from 40-115euros per night, depending on your preference of room. Alnog with breakfast and wifi, the staff can issue vehicle passes to enter Perugia's center.

Hotel Fortuna
Hotel Fortuna is a three star hotel located close to Corso Vennucci, in Perugia's old town center. This hotel has an elegant interior, with frescoed walls and divinely decorated suites. Continental breakfast comes included with your stay, and is served in their 14th century styled breakfast room. With prices starting at 45 euros for a triple, the

staff ensures to provide its guests with superior hospitality as well as inform them on the current events happening around the city.

What to do in Perugia on a Day Visit

Got only one day in Perugia before continuing your travels elsewhere? Wandering what to see in only one day? No problem, you can still get the best of the city between sun-up and sun-down. Starting from the 36 hours in Perugia by the NY Times we created our own insider guide to visit Perugia in one day. Conceived for students who are doing budget travel in Italy and don't want to spend too much time inside museums.

Below is our step-by-step guide to the perfect day in Perugia.

Towards the Sky: From the train station you've made your way up, up, up with Perugia's light rail, the MiniMetrò.

Take the elevator up and drink in that view, then walk twenty steps to Living Café, and drink it in some more while you sip your <u>cappuccino.</u> You've got a great day ahead of you, but you need to caffeinate to fit it all in.

Museum...or not: Follow the crowd of MiniMetrò riders out the arch into Via Oberdan, which takes you to Piazza Matteotti, parallel to Perugia's main drag, Corso Vannucci. Take any street up to the corso and walk towards the fountain. Here you can either a) check out the <u>National Gallery</u> (think Madonna and Child times a hundred and four) or head down to <u>San Francesco</u>. If you're into all things artey, the entrance is under the duel gryphons and three saints that adorn the side entrance to the town hall.

If you're not in the mood for frescoes, look for the big clock on the side of the town hall, just to the left of the gallery's entrance. Under it is Via dei Priori: if you walk all the way down you'll pass through a nice neighborhood and near the bottom (go right before the big arch!), the church of <u>San Francesco</u> in the Meadow. It's a nice green lawn where Perugians hang out and sunbathe. Walk back up and sit on the Steps of the cathedral and people-watch for a while.

Filling Your Belly: Hungry yet? Instead of sitting down in a restaurant somewhere, do as the Perugini do—eat on the Steps!!! For <u>lunch on the Steps</u>, we recommend one of Perugia's three main food groups (for students): a panino, a pizza to-go, or a kebab. For a <u>panino</u>: la Bottega di Perugia in Piazza Morlacchi facing the Duomo, go left and then turn right, follow the street until your reach Piazza Morlacchi. The paninis are great quality

AND the cheapest. The owner and his son are the friendliest people, immediately making you feel at home. For <u>pizza to-go</u>: check out Pizza Mediterranea (around the side of the cathedral but head right into the other small parking lot/piazza, Piazza Piccinino) and ask for your pizza "da portare via" to get the take out box instead of a table. <u>For a kebab</u>: Try the first going down in via Ulisse Rocchi.

The Aqueduct: After you've enjoyed your meal on the steps (and gotten a bit sunburned), make your way to the Aqueduct to get some leisurely exercise. Get up from the steps and walk to the right, past the fountain, and keep making right until you're in Via Baldeschi, then keep your eyes peeled on the left for a steeply-descending street called Via Appia. Head down and then onto Via dell'Acquedotto, which used to bring an aqueduct that brought water to the fountain. Enjoy the walk on the aqueduct, and remember this is a stroll not a sprint. Beauty is not lost on the Italian people, nor should it be lost on you.

The University of Gelato: Eventually the Aqueduct will end. Take a right in Via Fabretti and walk a hundred yards back to Piazza Fortebraccio. The large pink building to your right is the University for Foreigners. If you aren't too tired, pretend you are supposed to be there and keep going up to the top of the building for an amazing view. You've reached the summit, but for a little bit of heaven (aka gelato), you'll need to descend.

Chocolate: One of Perugia's best gelato shops is Augusta Perugia, located 30 seconds' walk from the university on Via Pinturicchio (on the far side of the basketball court and up the first little stairs). Augusta Perugia also sells chocolate, if you're looking to try some of the native wares. They produce their own chocolate, packaged in boxes with cool old paintings of Perugia. Good for a nice, inexpensive present

The...Church: You may still have your gelato in your hand now (we doubt it), but head back to the piazza where the university is and up through the Etruscan Arch (built 2,300 years ago!). Go back to Corso Vanucci. It's now time to venture into the cathedral and the Town Hall of Perugia, both in Piazza IV Novembre. From outside the cathedral seems has won the "Ugliest Cathedral in Italy" contest for four years running, but the inside is really...baroque. Go for Ba-roque and take a look! Actually inside you can find various art including the Moretti-Caselli stained glass windows, the Holy Ring, apparently (*very* apparently) the relic of the wedding ring of the Holy Virgin and the *Deposition from the Cross* by Federico Barocci. Cross the piazza to the main entrance of the town hall (look for the bronze gryphon and lion): this is where the nobles got together to figure out how to screw over the peasants a bit more. Check out the vaults! Now sit down at the café in the Piazza and relax.

Whisper Words of Love: And now for a bit of fun: the Whispering Arches. Go down Corso Vanucci to the end and cross the square of Piazza Italia. The big building on the far side of the piazza with the Gryphon on top is the Provincial building. Go under the arcade under the building's corner: have one person stand in the corner of the arch, facing the wall with their head tilted slightly upwards. Have another person do the same diagonally across and then whisper something to the wall. Pretty neat!

Rocca Paolina: When you've had enough fun with the arches, you'll notice you're quite close to an escalator. Curious? It leads to the old city, one buried when a vindicative pope razed this neighborhood to build a huge fortress, not to defend Perugia but to keep the rebellious Perugians in line. Where you're walking used to be the streets of a medieval neighborhood (look for doors and windows in the walls). Come back up and angle around the back of the building. Walk through the park and go to the great viewpoint:

Dinner dal Mi' Cocco: Finally, you must be hungry for dinner before you head home. If you want a real Perugian experience with great food, look no further than Dal Mi' Cocco, in Corso Garibaldi just a stone's throw from the University for Foreigners and the Etruscan Arch. They offer a set menu of several courses for only 13 euro, 15 with wine. The abundant meal includes home-made pasta and gnocchi, traditional meat dishes, and salad. if you're vegetarian just tell them "sono vegetariano" and they will bring you an omelets. If you want more of your courses, simply ask and, if they have extra, they'll give it to you.

Cappella di San Severo

Before young Raphael Sanzio made a name for himself in Florence and Rome, he settled briefly in Perugia, where in 1504 he painted the first of the many frescoes that would make him famous in his own lifetime and establish for him a place alongside Leonardo da Vinci and Michelangelo in the triumvirate of great Renaissance masters.

Only the upper half of his "Holy Trinity" remains, and that is damaged, and the work seems touchingly modest compared to the complex and engagingly humane "School of Athens" and other works he did for the Vatican palaces and chapels. As energetic in life as he was in his work, Raphael ran a huge workshop, had dozens of wealthy patrons, was in line to be a cardinal, and died on his 37th birthday, allegedly after a long, lustful session with his mistress. After Raphael's death, his then-septuagenarian teacher, Perugino, painted the six saints along the bottom of the fresco.

Casa del Cioccolato Perugina

Some 3km (2 miles) southwest of Perugia, the Casa del Cioccolato is the home of Perugia's iconic chocolate factory. The creator of Baci ("kisses") started in 1907 selling sugared almonds and now pumps out 120 tons of the brown stuff a day, including 1 1?2 million gianduja-and-hazelnut kisses. The site includes the Museo Storico Perugina, a small museum, where you can learn about the company's products and key moments in its history it was purchased by Nestlé in 1988 including an actual-size reproduction of the world's biggest chocolate, the BaciOne. Weighing in at

5,980kg, the monster choc was made in 2003 for the Eurochocolate festival, and apparently wolfed down by the crowds in just 4 hours.

To take a far more enjoyable factory tour, you'll need to phone and make reservations in advance English tours are available, but call to check times during the hours listed below. Guides run through the museum before leading groups on a walkway loop above the vast factory floor. Tours used to be free, but considering the piles of free chocolate on offer at the end (you can literally eat as much as you like), the new charge is probably justified. A gift store selling all the products rounds off the experience. *Note:* The factory shuts down production May through July (domestic demand drops off in the summer), so you won't see any activity in the factory at this time. The complex occasionally opens on Saturdays, but always confirm in advance. Call also about classes (from 1 hr. and up) at the on-site School of Chocolate.

Casa Museo di Palazzo Sorbello

Just around the corner from the cathedral, this historic home provides a rare window into 18th-century Perugia. The mansion dates back to the 16th century, though it was purchased by the aristocratic Marchesi Bourbon di Sorbello in 1785, and is lavishly furnished with period furniture. Ornate frescoes, a library of aging tomes, and the family's rare porcelain collection round out the experience.

Cattedrale di San Lorenzo

For a major Italian city and provincial capital, Perugia has a pretty disappointing cathedral, at least from the outside. First raised in the early 14th century on the Gothic model of the German hall churches, it didn't take its present form until the 16th century. Unsure whether the front on Piazza Danti or the flank facing Piazza IV Novembre should be the facade, Perugians slapped a bit of desultory decoration on both.

The interior is a bit gaudy (those columns are painted, not real marble), but there is a handful of good paintings. The first chapel on the left aisle is the Cappella del Sant' Anello, where a gilded reliquary protected by 15 locks supposedly holds the wedding ring of the Virgin Mary, stolen from Chiusi in 1473. Church officials solemnly take out the ring set with a pale gray agate whose color they swear changes, mood-ring style, to reveal the character of the person wearing it to show the crowds on July 29 and 30.

In the Cappella di San Bernardino (first on the right aisle) is baroque painter Frederico Barocchio's finest work, a tumultuous *Descent from the Cross* painted in 1567. Against the third pillar of the right aisle is the *Madonna della Grazie,* whose hallowed status is given away by dozens of ex-votos and burning candles surrounding it. It's attributed to Perugino's early-16th-century student Giannicola di Paolo. Just beyond it on the right aisle, in the Cappella del Sacramento, Luca Signorelli's 1484 *Madonna* altarpiece is provisionally installed.

The cathedral cloisters and former clergy dorms contain the mildly interesting Museo Capitolare (tel. 075 5720-4853; adults 3.50€, 2.50€ 12 to 26 years and 65 and over 65; free for children 12 and under), open Tuesday to Sunday 10am to 12:30pm and 3 to 5:30pm (use the separate entrance on the far corner of Piazza IV Novembre at no. 6), with its collection of rare religious artifacts, paintings by Luca Signorelli and Benedetto Bonfigli, and

Etruscan/Roman funerary art excavated from the city's ancient necropolis.

Galleria Nazionale

The world's largest repository of Umbrian art covers seven or so fruitful centuries and showcases dozens of artists, among whom two stand out in particular. Pride of place belongs to the altarpieces by Perugino, who was born nearby in Città della Pieve and spent much of his career working in Perugia, between time in Florence, where he studied alongside Leonoardo da Vinci, and in Rome, where he executed frescoes in the Sistine Chapel. Among his works in Rooms 22–26 are delicate landscapes, sweet Madonnas, and grinning Christ childs that reveal his spare, precise style. They are all the more ironically transcendent given that Perugino was openly anti-religion, and they certainly reveal nothing of the artist's fairly turbulent life—he was arrested in Florence for assault and battery and barely escaped exile; sued Michelangelo for defamation of character; and more than once was censored for reusing images and lacking originality. He persevered, however, and worked prodigiously until his death at age 73 and left a considerable fortune.

The museum's other showpiece is by a Tuscan, Piero della Francesca, who completed his "Polyptych of Perugia" for the city's church of Sant'Antonio in 1470. The symmetry, precise placement of figures and objects, and realistic dimensions of interior spaces reveal the artist's other occupation as a mathematician, though his figures are robustly human, real flesh and blood. The artist works sheer magic at the top of the piece, in a scene of the Annunciation, when an angel appears to Mary to tell her she will be the mother of the son of God. She's standing in a brightly lit cloister, and the illusion of pillars leading off into the distance is regarded as one of the greatest examples of perspective in Renaissance art.

Nobile Collegio del Cambio

The cubicles and fluorescent lighting of modern office life will seem all the more banal after a visit to the frescoed and paneled meeting rooms of Perugia's Moneychanger's Guild, one of the best-preserved "office suites" of the Renaissance. Perugino was hired in 1496 to fresco the Sala dell' Udienza (Hearing Room), perhaps with the help of his young student Raphael. The images merge religion, with scenes of the Nativity and Transfiguration; classical references, with female representations of the virtues; and most riveting of all, glimpses of 15th-century secular life that provide a fascinating look at Perugians of the time and their sartorial tastes.

Palazzo dei Priori

One of the largest town halls in Italy, this *palazzo* was started in the 1290s and expanded in 1443. Inside are the Collegio del Cambio and the Galleria Nazionale . The far end of the building has the oldest facade, with an off-center main portal (opposite the cathedral), from which spills a fan of steps. At their top are a small terrace and the *palazzo*'s first entryway, topped by bronze copies of the Perugian griffin and the Guelph lion. Through the door is the Sala dei Notari, a long rectangular room supported by eight large arches, formerly a citizens' assembly chamber and now used for public lectures and concerts. Matteo Tassi repainted much of it in 1860 with the coats of arms of Perugia's *podestà* (mayors) from 1297 to

1424, but in the spandrels of the arches remain the Old Testament and mythological scenes painted in 1297 by a follower of the Roman master Pietro Cavallini.

Pozzo Etrusco (Etruscan Well)

When the 3rd-century-B.C. Etruscans needed water, they sank a 5.4m-wide (18-ft.) shaft more than 35m (115 ft.) into the pebbly soil under Perugia. To support the cover over the well, they built two massive trusses of travertine that have stood the test of more than 2,000 years. You can climb down past the dripping, moss-smothered walls to a bridge across the bottom.

San Bernardino and San Francesco

The grassy lawn at the bottom of the Via dei Priori, a lounging spot for university students on sunny days, is bordered by two of the finest church facades in Perugia. On the left is the small Oratorio di San Bernardino, whose facade is layered with bas-reliefs and sculptures (created 1457-61, and beautifully restored in the 1990s) by Florentine sculptor Agostino di Duccio. Inside are a 1464 processional banner by Benedetto Bonfigli and a carved 4th-century paleo-Christian sarcophagus serving as the altar. The oratory's lumbering big brother next door is 13th-century San Francesco al Prato, with an unusual, vaguely Moorish geometric facade. It is undergoing a lengthy restoration and currently closed, but will eventually serve as a concert space.

San Pietro

This Benedictine monastery at Perugia's edge, its pointed Gothic tower a city landmark, was founded in the late 900s. Inside the first courtyard is the Romanesque entrance to the monastery's

San Pietro church. The church's old facade was uncovered in the 1980s, revealing 14th-century Giottesque frescoes between the arches the enthroned three-headed woman on the right may represent the Holy Trinity. The 16th-century interior is supported by ancient granite and marble columns (pilfered from a pagan temple) and is heavily decorated wallpapered with 16th-and 17th-century canvases, frescoed with grotesques, and filled with Renaissance and baroque paintings. The first altarpiece on the right is a colorful 16th-century *Madonna with Saints* by Eusebio da San Giorgio. Toward the end of the right aisle is the door to the sacristy (track down a monk to open it), which contains five small Perugino paintings of saints that were stolen in 1916 but found their way back here by 1993. Also here are two small Caravaggiesque works: The *Santa Francesca Romana with an Angel* is attributed by some to

Caravaggio himself, and the *Christ at the Column* copperplate sketch is a copy, perhaps of a lost Caravaggio original.

Ask the sacristan also to light up the choir so you can see the incredible wooden choir stalls, some of the finest examples of wood intarsia in all of Italy, produced in 1526 by a workshop under the direction of Bernardino Antonibi and Stefano Zambelli. In 1536, Stefano's brother Fra' Damiano inlaid the masterpiece door at the back, whose panels could hold their own against any painting of the Renaissance.

At the altar end of the left aisle are a strikingly medieval Pietà scene painted by Fiorenzo di Lorenzo in 1469 and paintings of *St. Peter* and *St. Paul* attributed to Il Guercino. The Cappella Vibi houses a gilded marble tabernacle by Mino da Fiesole, and in the Cappella Ranieri next door hangs Guido Reni's *Christ in the Garden.* Continuing down the left aisle, before the third altar, is another Eusebio da San Giorgio painting, this one of the *Adoration of the Magi* (1508). Between the second and first altars is a late *Pietà* by Perugino.

Museums in Perugia

The Casa Museo Palazzo Sorbello, Studio Moretti Caselli, and Giuditta Brozetti are historically significant to the city of Perugia and the Umbrian Region. These three museums have the same purpose: to preserve their traditions, to inspire appreciation for the Italian culture, and to encourage the understanding of its history. In these places, visitors are able to observe change throughout time by their collections and crafts, see the ingenuity of the women, and examine the physical structures that project their own stories.

We invite you to marvel, wander, and reflect the experience of being thrown back in time and see Perugia as it was in the past.

Tour Route

- ✓ From Studio Moretti Caselli to Casa Museo Palazzo Sorbello: 10-15 minutes walking distance

- ✓ From Casa Museo Palazzo Sorbello to Giuditta Brozzetti Museo Laboratorio: 15-20 minutes walking distance

- ✓ Tour Duration of 3 Museums: 2 hours 30 minutes

- ✓ note: tours may be split to two or more days

The building that now contains the Studio Moretti Caselli was one of the houses of the influential Baglioni Family of Perugia in the 1500s. Evidence of the family's wealth can be seen on the frescoed arches that remains in the studio to this day. Francesco Moretti converted this once stately home into his studio in 1859 and started his business in the art of creating stained glass. The business, along with its traditions and techniques, has been passed down through the generations. The current owners, Elisabetta and Maddalena Forenza, are only the most recent in a long line of female artists. The original techniques used by Moretti are still used but continue to adapt to modern methods.

In the museum, the important works from the past centuries are displayed along with sketches and machinery of the 20th century. One of the most notable items is the hand-painted portrait of Queen Margherita by Francesco Moretti completed in 1881.

Contact Information

Maddalena Forenza

Via Fatebenefratelli 206121 Perugia, Italy

Phone: +39 0755720017

Reservations: +39 340 7765594

The Casa Museo Palazzo Sorbello is the only house museum in Umbria. It was the residence of the influential noble family, Marchesi Ranieri Bourbon di Sorbello. Over time, the family accumulated a variety of collections that correspond to the different interests of members of the family. The museum, with its broad array of artifacts, represents the cultural memories and feelings of the inhabitants.

One of the most important collections is the historical library which contains an assortment of literature including the 1770 edition of the Encyclopedie Francaise by Diderot and D'Alembert. There is an extensive art collection consisting of paintings from prominent Italian and foreign artists as well as various unique porcelain sets, consisting of: a complete Ginori table service from the 18th century and an original Chinese table service dating back to the Qianlong period. Along with these collections, there is a room dedicated to the Marchesa Romeyene Robert and the Ranieri di Sorbello School of Embroidery, which employed the inventive historic technique known as the Umbrian Point, now known as the Sorbello Point.

Contact Information
Uguccione Ranieri di Sorbello Foundation

P.zza Piccinino, 9 06122 Perugia, Italy

Phone: +39 075 5732775

Email: promoter@fondazioneranieri.org

The Giuditta Brozzetti Museo Laboratorio di Tessitura Manuale was founded in 1921 by Giudittta Brozzetti and is one of the few remaining hand-weaving workshops in Italy today. The technique of creating textiles is a family tradition that has been handed down through four female generations. The textiles continue to be woven on wooden Jacquard looms, which were prominent in the beginning of the 19th century. In modern society, textiles and fabric are often mass produced so the Giuditta Brozzetti Museo Laboratorio represents a life before industry and the value of handmade products.

The museum/laboratory is located in the first Franciscan church in Perugia, built around the year 1212. It later known as the Women's Church of Saint Francis after being passed on to the Benedictine Sisters of Sant'Angelo. After changing hands several times, it was eventually realized as a workshop for hand-made textiles.

Contact Information
Marta Cucchia

Via Tiberio Berardi, 5/6 06123 Perugia, Italy

Phone: +39 07540236

Fax: +39 07541656

Mobile: +39 3485102919

Transport in Perugia

Buses >

City buses are generally reliable and relatively cheap. You get seventy minutes of riding; so if you have only a quick errand, try to get back on before it expires (the time is stamped on it). Riding black (i.e. without a ticket) is chancy and will net you a hefty fine if you're caught, so don't risk it. One biglietto (ticket) or corsa semplice, costs €1,50. If you forget, go immediately to the driver it will cost you €2 on board. A ten-ride ticket (*biglietto da dieci corse*) is slightly discounted, so get one if you'll be in town for a while. More than the slight discount, these tickets are useful because you're not always running to find a ticket from a tabaccaio when the bus is arriving you just hop on. You can also use the ticket for more than one person; just put it back in as soon as it's stamped. For local buses from Piazza Italia: check the map at the end of this guide or ask someone at the ticket booth, which line to take for your destination. APM also has a map for the whole bus network like the one for the London Tube. You can get it at the biglietteria on Piazza Italia.

Bus stands usually have both a map that shows the route of the bus (you are at the red dot) and a schedule of when the bus is planned to pass. Note that feriale means, 'work days' (Saturday usually included, though some schedules now have feriale and sabato feriale) and festivo means, 'Sundays and public holidays.' The buses always have their destinations (make sure you know what direction you are heading) on the electronic display at the front, and some have displays inside of upcoming stops. The principal nodes where buses connect are at Piazza Italia, Piazza Partigiani (where the long-distance buses arrive), Piazza Morlacchi or Cavallotti (below the fountain), and Piazza Grimana (by the University for Foreigners). If you ask a driver nicely and stick close to the front, she'll likely let you know when your stop is up. Just say: "Vorrei scendere a…………"

Don't get confused by "alternate" buses: G1 and G2 have substantially the same route but different final destinations, while the TS and TD both do the same loop but in opposite directions! You can get an orario (timetable) of all the buses at the stand on Piazza Italia; it's a different one for the summer. Look in the back to find the timetable for the festivi. Remember that when you're waiting for the bus, you have to stick out your hand to tell the driver that you want him to stop for you. You can find the schedules for both the local buses and the long-distance buses run by APM online at www.apmperugia.it. Look at the left under Orari. On the orari page you will see an option to look at the urban bus lines of Perugia and other cities (i.e. the yellow buses), while below you'll see the line for the extraurbani (long-distance) schedules. Select which line you want, remembering that feriale means Monday-Saturday.

MiniMetrò > Perugia's light rail line finally opened on 29 January 2008, and boy are we proud of it! The Stazione Pincetto is the one near the Mercato Coperto in the center, and trains leaving from Stazione Pincetto head towards the train station (Stazione Fontivegge), the Questura (Stazione Cortonese) and the Saturday Market, Percorso verde, and stadium (Stazione Pian di Massiano).

To get to the Stazione Pincetto, walk from Piazza Matteotti at the opposite end from the Coop, down Via Oberdan to number 18. Look for the blue Minimetrò "M" and the word "Pincetto" on your left. Go down the alley, down the walkway, and down the escalators to the station.

The MiniMetrò is open Mo-Sa 7-21:20, Sunday and holidays 8:30-20:30, though the last run starts fifteen minutes before closing. Transport in Perugia is now "unified" in the sense that the standard "UP" ticket is valid for the urban network made up by the various means of public transport (Minimetrò-APM-ACAP-RFI-FCU). The tickets are available at automatic dispensers (you can even pay by Creditcard) at the entrance of each MiniMetrò station, as well as at authorized dealers (newsstands, the tabaccaio, some cafés).

Cars > Can You Drive Like An Italian? Those that have a car in Perugia are both benedetti and maledetti (blessed and cursed). On one hand it makes reaching a lot of picturesque Umbrian cities and attractions like the hot springs much easier. On the other hand the limited traffic (and even more limited parking) in the center make a car a headache. Rental is easy, but note that when renting a car in Italy it's next to impossible to find a car that's automatic. It's safe to say that if you don't drive with manual gears, you probably won't be able to rent a car in Italy. Here are some options: Avis There is an office at the main train station (Stazione F.S.) Maggiore This is also down next to the train station. These guys have a reputation for renting you a car without a lot of hassle, even if you're younger than 25 years old. Just take your passport and a credit card and usually they will help you out. 075.500.7499. Hertz Once again, just to the right of the train station. It's a family-run place and they have a cute little poodle named Golia (Goliath). Call 075.500.2439 for more info.

A word on the ZTL and Parking: To make the center more pedestrian-friendly, Perugia, like many Italian cities, has created a *zona traffico limitato*, a Limited Traffic Zone. The precise hours depend on the time of the year and are listed in the back of the city's infobrochure VivaPerugia. The TI has a small guide for parking, Guida ai parcheggi della città, which describes the pay parking lots well and only puts a little blue P (no box around it) on its map for the free parking spots. You can get the tourist ticket for parking at Piazza Partigiani: only €7.75 for twenty-four hours. Ask at the cash register right after you park.

Fancy sharing a ride? If your lingo is bello you can try hooking a hitch through the dedicated Italian site, www.postoinauto.it. Don't ask us: any arrangements you make are completely between you and Guido. If from a neighboring country, e.g. Germany, you might as well look on the home country sites you are familiar with. You might find somebody who can take you all the way home to Mutter.

Transportation outside Perugia

Extra-urban transport: Buses, Trains, Taxi, Flights

Trains >

Just to start off right, buses R and TS go to the station from Piazza Italia. Italy's train system, despite privatization, remains excellent and relatively cheap compared with the rest of Europe. No, it seems you don't need a fascist government to make the trains run on time. However, those traveling by train should be sure to get to the station at least an hour ahead of time, just in case. You can get info at the station but you can also buy a schedule (*orario)* for the trains for €4 at any newsstand. The computerized information kiosks generally work very well, if they work. Trenitalia's site is also moron-easy to use:

www.trenitalia.com (and also has an English version). There's also the FCU, the Umbrian Central Line, a separate railway with its own little station, "Perugia Sant'Anna," not too far from Piazza Partigiani. This makes a number of the smaller cities much more accessible: Umbertide, Città di Castello, Terni, Todi, and Marsciano. Often ignored by foreigners, the Umbrian Central Railroad is Trenitalia's forgotten little sister no more! Other than getting you to Ponte San Giovanni to shop, the FCU takes you to all the little Umbrian cities that your mother never told you about. There's a line all the way to Aquila, too. In any event, the FCU is an inexpensive way to see Umbria. Check out the site at www.fcu.it. Traveling will be simpler if you understand how to read the timetables. In every train station there will be two of them one white, one yellow. The white ones are arrivals (arrivi) while the yellow ones are the departures (partenze). The schedule is organized chronologically. The columns are organized like this: first, the ora (time of departure). Second, the treno (train) type and number.

Note that a little squiggle like the Greek letter sigma means that the train is periodic (i.e. not every day). The train type is organized by color. Green is for the regional and interregional trains, the slower ones that make more stops. The faster diretti are black. InterCity (IC) and EuroCity (EC) are red, faster, and you'll need to buy a supplement in addition to the ticket. Finally, the super-quick EuroStar (ES) is in blue; a supplement and a reservation are mandatory. Also in this column you may find a little S in a circle; this means that this train runs even in case of a strike (sciopero). An R means that a reservation is helpful, an R in a box means it's obligatory. It's best to buy the schedule and learn how to use it, but in an emergency remember that there is a copy of the schedule in the escalator corridor in the Rocca Paolina.

The column with *principali fermate e destinazioni* (main stops and destinations) is the most important. The largest city is the destination and the time next to it is when it arrives there. There will also be listed some of the other destinations. "*Si ferma in tutte le stazioni*" means that this train stops at every stop. Those heading north may need to transfer at Terontola: those heading south at Foligno. Don't miss these transfers if you're not on a direct train. In the second-to-last section, servizi diretti e annotazioni, there are random notes. "*Si effettua…*" means that the train runs on these days (feriali is Mo-Sa, domenica is only Sunday, festivi is only Sunday and holidays). Some of the other stations this train stops in might be listed. Finally, binario (track) is the platform the train leaves from. You will have to specify whether you want a one-way (*solo andata*) or a return/round-trip (*andata e ritorno*) ticket.

If you're voyaging skid-row make sure to request *seconda classe* (second class). Some other notes on Perugia's train station. There is an information office opposite the ticket counter that specializes in international train travel the person inside may or may not be helpful if you ask about trips only within Italy. When standing in line, note when the sportello (counter) closes. It is terrible to get to the counter and have it close on you. The station has a luggage storage office (out the back door to Platform 1, turn left, around the corner at the end of the building), and a beautiful waiting room (sala d'attesa). The station also has a little café, a newsstand and pay-per-pee. Oh, and don't get excited when you hear the bells, which you might think would indicate an arriving train.

They usually ring like mad for ten minutes, and then stop. A couple minutes later the train arrives if you've said the right prayers. Always remember to validate your ticket(s) before you leave just stick them in the yellow machine. If you forget to validate a ticket and get on the train, write the date and the exact time as soon as you realize in pen on the back of the ticket, or better yet find the conductor and explain this to him or her. If you're running late and run into a long line just before your train leaves, hop on and go find the conductor and tell him or her that you have gotten on without a ticket ("Sono salito senza biglietto"). You may pay €32 extra but you'll be able to catch the train. The other strategy is to go into the edicola (newsstand) and buy a destination-less kilometer ticket, e.g. 100 km that will be enough to get you where you want to go. Remember, unless you want a joyride to Woop-Woop, those heading north may need to transfer at Terontola, those heading south at Foligno. Don't miss these transfers if you're not on a direct train.

Long-Distance Buses >
These are often referred to as "i pullman" in Italian. Some cities (Gubbio, Castiglione del Lago, Siena) are much easier to reach by bus than by train. Long-distance buses usually leave from the station at Piazza Partigiani. Start in Piazza Italia and go down the escalators on the right side of the Rocca Paolina. At the bottom of the escalators, turn left, walk down a bit, and jog right to the next set of escalators. Take them all the way down and go out the tunnel, straight down the sidewalk, and down the stairs. Cross the street and you're at the bus station. In any event, the ticket area is on your

left as you face it from the bottom of the last set of stairs. If you ask nicely, you may get the free schedule of all the buses from that office. There are a number of companies that operate from Piaza Partigiani.

You're most likely to go with the Sulga company, which runs the buses that go to Napoli (Naples), Firenze (Florence), Milano (Milan), Roma (Airport and the Tiburtina train station) and Rome (Tiburtina station), and Puglia, etc. On the Sulga site (www.sulga.it) select Orari delle corse on the left, then put in the city of departure and arrival. The SENA Company runs the bus to Siena. For the hours, look at their site, www.sena.it. Click on Orari e tariffe on the left side, then three quarters of the way down click on the link for "Toscana-Umbria-Lazio." The Spoletina bus company is the biggest operator in south-eastern Umbria. See www.spoletina.com for bus services from Spoleto to many places not directly linked to Perugia, e.g. Bevagna, Bastardo, Norcia, etc.

Planes >
For Fiumicino: If you go by train, ask the train station employee to give you a ticket to Roma Tiburtina (€11.10) and then from Roma Tiburtina to Fiumicino Aeroporto (€6). If you say "Perugia to Fiumicino" you'll pay €10.12 to Roma Termini and then an extortionary €11.50 from Termini to Fiumicino. But either way you have to connect in Rome. If your flight leaves early you will have to go the night before because you won't arrive in time with the bus or train. The airport is outside the city and so you will have to sleep there, either on the chairs by the arrivals area or at the Hilton (a pretty penny).

There are also several Fiumicino airport buses every day operated by the Sulga Company. They leave from Piazza Partigiani at 6:30, 8, and 9 on feriali; check their site for festivi times. It takes from three to three-and-half hours to get to Fiumicino and the airport is the last stop; don't get off at Roma Tiburtina. Get the newest schedule at the Piazza Partigiani bus office or online at www.sulga.it, and call 800.099.661 for reservations (not obligatory). It's €21 one-way. Finally, there's the Terravision bus company that runs a very efficient shuttle service from Roma Termini to both Fiumicino and Ciampino. On the site at www.terravision.it it tells you where you can buy the tickets and when the shuttle leaves. From the Roma Termini Station, go out the doors on the right side of the station (when you are inside it with the tracks to your back). This is Via Marsala; walk away from the tracks (left) and go to number 22 (the Royal Santina Hotel). To Fiumicino it costs €9 one-way, €17 there and back, and takes seventy minutes. The earliest shuttle leaves at 6:30 and arrives at the airport at 7:40.

For Ciampino: the Terravision shuttle costs €8 one-way, €13.50 there and back, and takes forty minutes. The earliest shuttle leaves at 4:30 and arrives at the airport at 5:10. It leaves from the same place the Fiumicino shuttle leaves. Ciampino airport is connected by shuttle bus to Ciampino railway station (reachable from Termini) and the stop Anagina on the metropolitana (subway system). Ryan Air also has its own shuttle but it is extortionary. Remember that Ryan Air strictly enforces the baggage weight and size limit (55 by 40 by 20 centimeters), so don't exceed it! Need to get to FCO or Ciampino at a weird hour, or need to arrive from there? Ask Student Living for special rates for individuals and groups to and from the airport.

Taxis >

There's a taxi stand in the corner of Piazza Italia. The beasts can also often be found lurking in Corso Vannucci in front of Palazzo dei Priori in Via Fani outside Merlin or in Piazza Italia next to the scale mobili, where there's even a callbox. Otherwise call the Perugia Taxi number on 075.500.4888. A ride from the train station to the center of Perugia costs about €9. Please note that rates are higher on Sundays and holidays. The taxis are now 24 hours so there is no need (or way) to reserve one just call.

Food and Drink

Cafes, Pubs, Bars

Pub entertainment schedules change as often as Italian political alliances so look out for flyers and posters to keep abreast of what's on. If you can manage to back-translate the mangled English of these documents into Italian it usually helps to understand what they are talking about. Most nightspots are desperate to pull a crowd so if you have a hot idea that you think might work, go ask them.

One day you too may be standing in front of the Uni for hours on end offering badly-written flyers to the unwashed.

Dempsey's > Dempsey's is the place to be to watch all of Perugia drink on the cheap and it's the easiest place to make friends. Be sure to introduce yourself to Andreas-your hard rock host. You wouldn't expect a man who likes bands with names like "Muncipal Waste" and "Cattle Decapitation" to be a *simpaticone*, but he's been voted Perugia's nicest guy four straight years. This is the place for the cheapest (and best quality) cocktail along the main street, or just hang out and have a beer before heading to the steps. Centrally located in Piazza Danti across from the front of the Duomo.

Elfo's Pub (the place to beer) > Best place for <u>craft beers in Perugia</u>. Although it's been through many incarnations, the actual sala of Elfo's is the oldest pub in Perugia, founded in the storied year 1968. It was a *circolo* (like a private club) for a while, then the first vegetarian restaurant in Perugia: in the '70s a now-famous zen monk handpainted its buddha on the wall. Luckily for all of us, it's now public. Go down via dei Priori a bit and take your second left into via Sant'Agata, to number 20. Enter and find a cozy sala (note the bike hanging-touch it for good luck) and good-natured manager Natale. You're here to relax and listen to rock with a capital R, dangit. They <u>have six different beers on tap as well as around 200 different beer (Belgian and America too!) in bottles</u>, all at very reasonable prices. Boasts the best Guinness in town, and is now serving Indian Pale Ale as well. Happy hour until 21:00 with a pint of your favorite blond at a special prices. <u>They also have a kitchen for fried stuff and panini.</u> Drop by every day of the week from 20-02:00. Oh, and that screen's for sports, too, so if you're feeling deprived of the NFL, look no further.

Caffè Morlacchi > I can't hear that name without thinking of the Morlocks from H.G. Wells' *The Time Machine*, but no little grey men will spirit you down to their underworld if you go there. It's an intimate if sometimes crowded place populated with teachers and students from the Faculty of Humanities just across the way. The owners are ready to make you up a great drink or share a laugh. Morlacchi gets cultural with poetry, quality concerts, and art exhibitions drop by to find out when. They have an aperitivo every day, with a dj or live music (often jazz and blues) on the weekends. Hannah's table is in front of the window in the front left but if she's not there you can have it. If you have a chance to stop by for a cappuccino in the morning, try their fantastic cornetto alla Nutella. Best in town. Predictably, it's at Piazza Morlacchi 8, open 8am-1am every day except Sunday, when hours are 5-10pm.

The Last Word > Mixology Bar with Arabic atmosphere; Here you can taste delicious cocktails prepared by experts while sitting on a swing hanging from the ceiling. It's in Via della Stella, 3 (off Piazza Morlacchi), open 6.30pm-1.30am

La Perla del Deserto > It's probably easier for a camel to pass through the eye of a needle than to recreate the ambience of an Arab teahouse in Italy. Despite the lighting, Mahmoud has made a reasonable job of it so far...like most things less than 2000 years old around here, it's a work in progress. Get stuck into Arab cakes like basbousa, assorted teas, fruity hubble-bubble pipes and Turkish coffee while you lounge with your harem (harem not provided) on the exotic cushionry. Belly dancing on Thursday evenings and Latin American Fridays. Closed Mondays, otherwise open 18:00-02:00 at Corso Garibaldi 106, 075.947.2299

Reset > Italians would crawl miles over broken pottery to drink good coffee, so don't bellyache to me that reset is a bit out of town. 20 minutes' walk away at Via d'Andreotti (go down via Pascoli next to Gallenga and keep on goin') gets ya summa dat joe wid giò. Lots of shiny bits, fancy lounges, chic styling and even a red carpet entrance. Exotic beers as well and outdoor tables for the cigaretterie. Glam it up, baby boo.

Kandinsky Pub > This place is half artsy, half funky, the pub of Perugia's leftwing scene, but also its goofballs. Silvia likes it and so did I, from the moment I saw the art nouveau lettering on the outside. It's at Via Enrico dal Pozzo 22. To get there, go to Porta Pesa and drop a small rubber ball. It will roll across the intersection and down Via xiv Settembre (towards Palazzina Prosciutti, for students at the University for Foreigners). Just ten metres from Porta Pesa, go left down the metal stairs; at the bottom go straight and then your second left. Kandinksy is named for a famous russian expressionist and shows it there's lots of art on its multicolored walls, as well as lots of artsy Italians.

Lacio Drom (ex "Il birraio") > One of Perugia's claims to fame, this classy place is in all the quality guidebooks. At the birraio the beer's brewed fresh in the huge copper kettles you can see inside the door. It has a relaxed atmosphere unlike most of the city's subterranean pubs, there are even windows with a great view. They also have a large room downstairs, complete with eclectic furnishings and even more of that great beer (though you'll find fine wines and cocktails if you wish). From behind the duomo, take the middle road (the only one that rises), Via del Sole, and don't stumble off to the right. It's almost at the end on the left (number 18 after the street turns into Via delle Prome). Open every day but Monday, 20-02:30. Be sure to check out the birthday book on the left as you enter the bar.

Italian Food Culture

Simply put, Italians love food. The ceasefire of commercial hostilities in the middle of the day is largely so that everyone can go home and have a rollicking-good lunch. Various kinds of food cultivation and production have been part of the physical landscape for thousands of years, becoming deeply ingrained upon the psyche. Food is feted and celebrated, newspapers carry olive oil reviews, mention of a classic dish brings an appreciative murmur in almost any social situation.

Breakfast almost does not exist in Italy. At home most Italians have a large bowl of warm milk with a squirt of coffee in it and biscuits or a croissant. In a coffee bar it might be one of the myriad styles of coffee with a custard-filled brioche or light pastry.

We've actually written a short essay on the subject, the "Little Green All-About-Caffeine", but this could be an encyclopedia.

Our best coffee advice is to observe what Italians order, learn the names of the coffee variations and try them when you feel adventurous.

Lunch is the main game and can have several courses, typically one of pasta and one of meat, along with vegetable side-dishes, salad, bread and wine. Dinner is much the same thing and can be extended with an antipasto such as bruschetta, soup, dessert, coffee, digestives and fruit.

Italians say *siamo alla frutta* (we're at the fruit) to indicate that they have almost finished something; if it's the end of an Italian meal, it might have been a long road indeed! Decoding your dinner menu doesn't require the help of Da Vinci. The order is *antipasto* (little cuts of meat and cheese, usually, as an appetizer), then a *primo* (usually a pasta dish), a *secondo* (usually meat dishes) and *contorno*(cooked vegetables on the side), then *dolce* (dessert), *caffé* (you know this one), and maybe even a *digestivo* (also called an *amaro*), a bitter little liquor drunk (supposedly) to help you digest your meal. Remember that you are not obligated to buy each course, or even in the Italian order. As for restaurants, Italians have a classification of *tavola calda* (the place keeps things hot and it may be buffet style), *taverna* (tavern-style), *osteria* (simple restaurant, possibly cheaper), and *ristorante* (where you can expect all the courses, and usually more expensive).

Wine is the accompaniment par excellence to the food of Umbria. Wine-production has taken place in the region since Etruscan times and is still an important industry today. Various types of wine within Italy are classified into doc labels where only those made to a certain formula and style are entitled to identify with traditional names.

Vegetarians please note that animal fat, often pig fat, is used in the preparation of some cakes and breads. If you are particular about this then avoid products containing *strutto* and *lardo*. Ask to see the list of ingredients if in doubt.

Have allergies? Use the following phrase with the appropriate word at the end: *io sono allergico...* *alle noci* (nuts)...*alle fragole*(strawberries)...*al pepe* (pepper)...*ai frutti di mare* (seafood)...*al glutine* (gluten)... *agli idioti* (morons).

Here we present some common terms, though remember that Italians frequently use the preposition a where we would use with: *linguine al pesto* would be linguine with pesto sauce, while *penne all'arrabbiata* means penne with hot sauce (literally "angry penne!").

Restaurants & Pizzerias

Where to eat in Perugia? We've tried to include both cheap eats and really nice, slightly more expensive places, as well as where to go when you're sick of Pasta.

Also Before going to a restaurant check out and print our Italian Menu Dictionary

Italian Restaurants

Bottega del Vino > High quality Umbrian dishes, wide selection of Italian wines, amazing cheesecake, and great service. The atmosphere is intimate, good for a nice date or an evening out with friends. They have live jazz every Wednesday. If you're worried about price, just go for the wine or the cheesecake and browse the menu. You'll be back. Via del Sole 1, 075.571.6181. €€

La Taverna > One of Perugia's best known and best loved restaurants. Known for the fresh, delicious food, the helpful staff, and the charming and skilled chef.

<u>Al Mangiar Bene</u> > Delicious local and organic food ranging from pizzas to typical Umbrian *primi* and *secondi.* Davide, Renato, and Company buy directly from the farmers, so there's no middleman. You can see where the food comes from on their site, www.almangiarbene.com. Open for lunch and dinner Monday-Saturday on Via della Luna 21. Call 075.573.1047 for reservations. €€

<u>Osteria a Priori</u> > This top-rated osteria is known for it's good Umbrian pastas, wines, and the upstairs seating for a bargain. Via dei Priori 39, 075.572.7098. €€

<u>Locanda Do' Pazzi</u> > Great food and great service, lots of locals here, too. Reasonable prices for delicious pastas, wines, and desserts. They have your traditional Umbrian truffles, but more innovative dishes to try, too. Corso Cavour 128, 075.572.0565. €€

<u>Ristorante Pizzeria Ferrari</u> **>** They have much more than pizza and with the location on Corso Vannucci (for outdoor seating), it's a good value for your money. There is a wide range of vegetarian options, too. Check out their partner "Lunabar" for aperitivo in the early evening, they supply a great buffet with one drink of 5-7€. Via Scura 1, 075.572.2966. €€

<u>Dal Mi Cocco</u> **>** A must! We made a special page for Dal Mi Cocco restaurant, Corso Garibaldi 12, 075.573.2511, €

Pizzerias

<u>Pizzeria Mediterranea</u> **>** One of our favorites because of their delicious, huge pizza pies, the venue, and the prices. Open for lunch and dinner, Piazza Piccinino 11/12 Da Antonio, 075.572.13.22.

<u>Pizza e Musica</u> **>** Everything, from the Neapolitan pizzaiolo Felice to the décor, is tranquillo. The

ingredients come straight from Napoli and the oven is wood-burning. Try the focaccia (pizza dough baked with olive oil, salt, and rosemary on top) as an appetizer, then eat one of their tasty pizzas. Open Monday-Saturday for lunch and dinner, Via della Madonna 5.

Quattro Passi al Merlin > Here English-speaking Gennaro offers you a long list of pizzas that, when they arrive at the table, cover your plate. You can also get delicious antipasto plates, salti in bocca, and calzoni (like pizza folded over and sealed-the name means "big sock"). At lunch you can choose one of five pizzas and a drink and take it away for €5. Discounts for foreigners. Open 12:30-14:45 and 19:30 to late, Tu-Su, Via del Forno (off Corso Vannucci), call 075.571.6120 for reservations or to order take-out.

<u>Pizzeria Etruschetto</u> > Delicious Neapolitan-style pizza you can get slices, order full pizzas for sit-down, or take away dining. If you're having a party or just have a big appetite, try the metre-long pizza. Sometimes more quantity doesn't mean less quality! Their hours are Mo, We, Th, Fr 12-14:30 and 18-24:00, Sa & Su 18-24:00, closed Tuesdays.

<u>Pizzeria Toscana</u> > Freshly baked slices for 1-2€, depending on the kind. I like to buy whatever he is pulling out of the oven. Off Corso Vannucci near Piazza Italia, look for the "Pizza al Taglio" sign.

Café's You Can't Miss

<u>Café Morlacchi</u> > This student favorite has a great atmosphere with a long bar and lots of tables and chairs. They always have posters for the Morlacchi Theater and cool artwork, too. Great place for breakfast, lunch, and meetings. Occaisionally they'll have aperitivo, too. Piazza Morlacchi.

<u>Pinturicchio Cafe+Kitchen</u> > Comfy couches, lots of students, and good wifi. Great place to grab a caffe and a croissant and sit for a while. Via Pinturicchio 26.

Macrobiotic

<u>Chicco Integrale</u> > (The Whole Kernel) has a macrobiotic lunch menu and a little store with tempeh, miso, and lots of other organic foods. It is in the corner of Piazza IV Novembre near Via della Gabbia look for the little sign on the door.

International Food

<u>Chinese: La Grande Muraglia</u> . Prices are reasonable and there's a student menu, which is €5 (Although you can't order it Saturdays, Sundays, or holidays). This place offers great value for your money. Via Pinturicchio 49. Call 075.572.3938 for pick up, or sit down for a nice meal.

<u>Greek: Il Greco</u> > Perugia's only Greek restaurant

luckily has great food, so if you're craving feta, stop by on Via Boncambi.

Middle Eastern: Kebab places> In 2003 Italy was part of a coalition that invaded Iraq. After 2003, Iraqis were part of a coalition of kebab shops that invaded Italy. You can find a kebab joint on most streets in Perugia, so keep an eye out if you're craving falafel.

Baba burgers and Food lab > Craving a great hamburger? New arrival in Perugia, Baba makes the best burgers in town...right in the center of Perugia. They also have vegetarian and fish burger option. They all get served with delicious potatoes. Baba also serves nice and rich salads as long pasta, meat dishes and desserts. Via Oberdan 35, 075.572.8454 . €€

Buying Food in Perugia

Super Markets >: A persistent Perugia myth is that the Coop at the train station is the best deal. Save your two €1.5 tickets on the MiniMetrò for a soccer game, and go to Metà, the handy supermarket located at Via Baglioni 7. They've got all your Day-That-Ends-In-"Y" needs, plus some. Nikos' pick: the Greek yoghurt in the deli section, for making tzaziki. Another option is Todis: if you want to shop more with less money, take bus number G to Via della Pallota (ask the bus driver to get off at Todis), where you will see the store to your right. There's also one in Monteluce. Take Via Brunamonti from Porta Pesa, make that huge right-hand turn and walk towards the big, church-like building (the old hospital): Todis is down behind the pharmacy on the left.

Markets >: The Mercato Coperto (Covered Market) is the best place to go, bar none. Before you arrive, a little history: Piazza Matteotti used to be

Perugia's marketplace, and if you look at the wall at number 21, you'll see the official medieval measurements carved in stone. Anyway, after the Second World War the city needed the street, so they built a huge tower outside the walls and moved the market there. Go through a little arch/tunnel at Number 18A to get to the terrace (notice that you cross a sort of drawbridge to the "tower"). Go to either side of the top floor to find the stairs down.

Another market not to be missed is the organic market on Piazza Piccinino, behind the duomo. It's the first Sunday of every month, 8-17:00. You can not only get produce but also bread, honey, soap, and all sorts of handicrafts. Remember, too, that all products sold at the market are made by their vendors, which guarantees the highest level of "authenticity" and transparency. An Umbrian delicacy to try here is *formaggio al tartufo*, a bold cheese flavored with black truffle.

Perugia's Saturday market is held in a vast car park adjacent to the Renato Curi soccer stadium. Take either Bus G from Piazza Italia or the MiniMetrò to Pian di Massiano. There's fresh fruit and vegetables, meat, fish, bread, clothes, manchester, shoes and other odds and ends. Hours are 8-13:00 all year round.

Specialty food>

Giò is a great specialties store that sells, wine, craft beers, special jams, cranberry juice, the widest selection of tea we have ever seen, special pasta, salts, and spices, mustard of all sorts, chocolate; but also tools to make sushi, specialty tahimi, packages to make tacos and even Jiffy peanut butter . The only problem is that it is not exactly cheap. It's in between the center and the train station in via Ruggero D'Andreotto, 19. You have to enter the building and you will see a nice grocery store called Conad; the Giò store is right next to it.

Spices >: Another hard thing to find: the right spice. Get all your curry and *garam masala* at Via dei Priori 15, the *Antica Spezieria e Drogheria Bavicchi*. It's been a Perugian institution for over a century and they have tons of spices as well as loose tea and legumes in bulk. Alan says the beans, even the expensive ones, are "beantastic." Go figure.

Alternative/Organic Food >: See the entries for Punto Macrobiotico above. Then there's also Bavicchi in P.Matteotti for wheatgrass, sprouts, and juicers. If you want organic, we wholeheartedly recommend Rita's little fruit-and-veggie shop at Via dei Priori 98, down just past the escalators, in the shadow of the Torre degli Sciri. Depending on the time of the year, almost all of the produce on the shelves is from Rita's garden, all 100% organic. "My hands are my [organic] guarantee", says Rita with a smile as she holds her palms out to you: yep, they're pretty calloused. She admits her hours are "*un po' sbandato*", but figure more or less 8:45-13:15 and 18:15-20:30. Check out the poem about Rita in Perugian dialect next to the cash register, too.

On Sundays >: It's Sunday and you realize that all you have to eat is 100g of pasta and an apple. Nikos and I used to walk all over Perugia looking for a grocery store that was open. Never fear, there are now three: the Alimentare Bangladesh at Via dei Priori 71 just a bit above the *scale mobili* as well as its sister store in Piazza Cavalotti, and the Chinese store at Via Fabretti 67. These places often have "ethnic ingredients" like tahini, curry, or peanut butter, if you come from a culture with more than four spices. Metà is also open on Sundays, as is the alimentare at Via Bartolo 12-14 (only until 13:00 though).

R. Ceccarani >: Italians love their pastries and deservedly so for there are some fantastic local specialties. Look out for the typical *torcolo,* a favorite Perugian almond-cake. One of the well-regarded establishments in the center of town is R. Ceccarani Panetteria e Pasticceria, next to the Coop in Piazza Matteotti at number 16. The service is fast, they have a great range and the stuff is always super fresh. Closed Sundays. It's mighty difficult to buy salted bread in this town without the express permission of the Grand Wazoo, but you can try asking for pane salato.

4AM >: It's the middle of the night and you're hungry. Bakeries, open at that hour to make their wares, often sell (slightly less than legally) their *cornetti* and pizza. Try the super-chipper Massimiliano at *Il Fornaio at Porta Pesa*, the bakery at the bottom of Via dei Priori, or Le Mille Delizie at the junction of Via XIV Settembre and Via del Conventuccio (near Corso Cavour).

Pasta Fresca >: An experience you shouldn't miss. As compared with the one-trick-pony dry pasta in every store, fresh pasta is made with eggs as well as durum wheat flour. Try the nice little old man at Via Caporali 3.

Vino Sfuso >: Bring your own container to the *vino sfuso* place Rosso Vino at Corso Garibaldi 21, right near the Etruschetto. Perfect for parties!

Alimentari >: These friendly little family-run grocery stories are a dying breed. The hole-in-the-wall likely has food that's a whole lot fresher and with your tomatoes and peaches you get recipes, too. Our pick is the one at the top of Via Bartolo, at numbers 12-14. The super-friendly Signore and his son and daughter (Daniele and Paola) will make your buying experience a happy one. Check out their sandwiches and other delicious foods under the glass at the bread counter!

Recipes

As far as we can see, the key to Italian cooking is using a small number of fresh ingredients. This simplicity allows you to taste each one individually as well as in concert. Plus, the dishes are not too hard to make. For people not familiar with British measurements, a "TBSP" is a large kitchen spoon, a "tsp" a small tea spoon, while a cup (C) is about the size of a waterglass. Italians tend to use the abbreviation "q.b." in their recipes, which stands for quanto basta, "as much as is enough." Another thing: always use extra virgin olive oil-it's a bit more expensive but better quality. If you want to learn more about Italian ingredients and specifically Umbrian ones, check out Alan's delectable essay, "Edible Jewels In The Umbrian Crown," archived and readily-downloadable here.

On the Little Blue Menu:

Panzanella Recipe

This is a way poor people used to use up stale bread. I admit my recipe isn't the classic one, but it's still good. The night before you want to make this dish, cut good white bread in cubes and put in a plastic bag (leave the bag open). The next day chop coarsely 6 large, ripe tomatoes and ½ of a small red onion. Add this and ¼ cup of chopped basil leaves to the plastic bag. In a small jar (an old jar cleaned out will do), make a vinaigrette: two parts olive oil to one part vinegar (balsamic is great for this!), plus salt, pepper, and whatever spices you want. Pour the vinaigrette into the plastic bag with the bread mixture, close the bag, and mix.

Panzanella Recipe

Prep time: 5 mins   Total time: 5 mins

This is a way poor people used to use up stale bread. I admit my recipe isn't the classic one, but it's still good.

- ➢ Ingredients
- ➢ white bread
- ➢ 6 large, ripe tomatoes
- ➢ of a small red onion
- ➢ cup of chopped basil leaves
- ➢ extra virgin olive oil
- ➢ vinegar (balsamic is great for this!)
- ➢ Salt, pepper and spices

Instructions

1. The night before you want to make this dish, cut good white bread in cubes and put in a plastic bag (leave the bag open).

2. The next day chop coarsely 6 large, ripe tomatoes and ½ of a small red onion.

3. Add this and ¼ cup of chopped basil leaves to the plastic bag.

4. In a small jar (an old jar cleaned out will do), make a vinaigrette: two parts olive oil to one part vinegar (balsamic is great for this!), plus salt, pepper, and whatever spices you want.

5. Pour the vinaigrette into the plastic bag with the bread mixture, close the bag, and mix.

Classic Tomato Sauce

Best in the summer and early fall when you can still get good tomatoes. Take 500g of plum tomatoes and cut them finely. Skin and dice finely a small onion. In a frying pan, sauté the onion in olive oil for five minutes, then add the diced tomatoes. Cook for a while, stirring frequently. Add a pinch of salt and some chopped basil leaves when you remove from heat. Add this to some spaghetti (spago means "string," so spaghetti means "little strings") cooked al dente, or just a little stiffer than normal.

Classic Tomato Sauce

Prep time: 5 mins   Cook time: 15 mins Total time: 20 mins

Serves: 4

Best in the summer and early fall when you can still get good tomatoes.

Ingredients

➢ 500g of plum tomatoes

➢ 1 small onion

➢ basil leaves

Instructions

1. Take 500g of plum tomatoes and cut them finely.

2. Skin and dice finely a small onion.

3. In a frying pan, sauté the onion in olive oil for five minutes, then add the diced tomatoes. Cook for a while, stirring frequently.

4. Add a pinch of salt and some chopped basil leaves when you remove from heat. Add this to some spaghetti (spago means "string," so spaghetti means "little strings") cooked al dente, or just a little stiffer than normal

Basic Dough

This dough can be used for both pizza and focaccia bread. In a large bowl mix 400g white flour (about 2 ½ cups) with 100g semolina flour (about 5/8 cups), then 1 tsp salt and 1 tsp sugar. Take 25g fresh brewer's yeast (lievito di birra look for the little yellow cubes), and dissolve it in a smallish cup of warm water. Once dissolved, pour slowly into the dry mix, adding 4 TBSP olive oil. Mix in more water slowly until you have a stretchy but not too dry mixture. If you add too much water, add more flour. Knead for 10-15 minutes, then put in a warmed up oven for 40-60 minutes. Take it out, knead again, adding some flour if it's sticky. Spread it out on a sheet: add olive oil, salt, and rosemary if it will be focaccia, tomato sauce and toppings for pizza. Cook for 30 minutes in an oven preheated to 180 Celsius.

Basic Dough

Prep time: 30 mins Cook time: 30 mins Total
time: 1 hour

This dough can be used for both pizza and focaccia
bread.

Ingredients

- ➢ 400g white flour (about 2 ½ cups)
- ➢ 100g semolina flour (about ⅝ cups)
- ➢ 1 tsp salt and 1 tsp sugar
- ➢ 25g fresh brewer's yeast (lievito di birra
  look for the little yellow cubes)
- ➢ 4 TBSP olive oil

Instructions

1. In a large bowl mix 400g white flour (about
   2 ½ cups) with 100g semolina flour (about
   ⅝ cups), then 1 tsp salt and 1 tsp sugar.

2. Take 25g fresh brewer's yeast (lievito di
   birra look for the little yellow cubes), and

dissolve it in a smallish cup of warm water. Once dissolved, pour slowly into the dry mix, adding 4 TBSP olive oil.

3. Mix in more water slowly until you have a stretchy but not too dry mixture. If you add too much water, add more flour.

4. Knead for 10-15 minutes, then put in a warmed up oven for 40-60 minutes. Take it out, knead again, adding some flour if it's sticky.

5. Spread it out on a sheet: add olive oil, salt, and rosemary if it will be focaccia, tomato sauce and toppings for pizza. Cook for 30 minutes in an oven preheated to 180 Celsius.

Tiramisu'

This word literally means "pick me up," so called because it has a lot of "energetic" ingredients in it. This recipe serves six. Separate 5 eggs. Whisk the 5 yolks and 150 grams of superfine confectioner's sugar (¾ cup, zucchero semolato) until pale. Fold in 500g mascarpone cheese (2 cups). In a separate bowl, beat until stiff the 5 egg whites with a bit of salt. Mix that into the egg yolk-sugar-mascarpone mixture. Spread a layer of this cream over the bottom of a large rectangular dish. Grate 200g of semi-sweet chocolate. Dip 30 Savoy biscotti (lady fingers) in 250 ml strong espresso (1 cup). Put down a layer of the biscotti, then another layer of the mascarpone mixture. Sprinkle the grated chocolate over the second cream layer. Put more biscuits down, then more cream, then more chocolate. Repeat, ending with a cream layer with 1 TBSP cocoa powder on top. Chill at least two hours before serving. Alan adds that all those layers may not be necessary; he can't remember ever seeing a tiramisù with more than three and unless you have a really deep dish only two layers is feasible.

Tiramisu'

Prep time: 30 mins Total time: 30 mins
Serves: 6

This word literally means "pick me up," so called because it has a lot of "energetic" ingredients in it.

Ingredients

- ➢ 5 eggs
- ➢ 50 grams of superfine confectioner's sugar (¾ cup, zucchero semolato)
- ➢ 500g mascarpone cheese (2 cups)
- ➢ 200g of semi-sweet chocolate
- ➢ 30 Savoy biscotti (lady fingers)
- ➢ 250 ml strong espresso

> ➤ 1 table spoon cocoa powder

Instructions

1. Separate 5 eggs. Whisk the 5 yolks and 150 grams of superfine confectioner's sugar (¾ cup, zucchero semolato) until pale.

2. Fold in 500g mascarpone cheese (2 cups).

3. In a separate bowl, beat until stiff the 5 egg whites with a bit of salt.

4. Mix that into the egg yolk-sugar-mascarpone mixture.

5. Spread a layer of this cream over the bottom of a large rectangular dish.

6. Grate 200g of semi-sweet chocolate.

7. Dip 30 Savoy biscotti (lady fingers) in 250 ml strong espresso (1 cup).

8. Put down a layer of the biscotti, then another layer of the mascarpone mixture.

9. Sprinkle the grated chocolate over the second cream layer. Put more biscuits down, then more cream, then more chocolate. Repeat, ending with a cream layer with 1 TBSP cocoa powder on top.

10. Chill at least two hours before serving.

11. Alan adds that all those layers may not be necessary; he can't remember ever seeing a tiramisù with more than three and unless you have a really deep dish only two layers is feasible.

Risotto

This fabulous rice dish is made in lots of different ways- here's a basic one. The idea with risotto is to add broth slowly to rice that's already been heated up, and to stir often, to bring out some of the rice's starch. This will give it sort of a creamy texture. On a side burner, bring 1 liter of water with 2 cubes of broth to boil. In a large frying pan, saute ½ onion, diced small, and 1 clove of garlic, minced. Add 1½ cups of arborio rice to the frying pan after three minutes and stir frequently for a few minutes. Pour in ½ cup of white wine (be careful of the steam), and then start adding the broth one cup at a time, stirring continuously. After several minutes, add ½ chopped fennel bulb. Keep stirring and adding broth until the rice is cooked. Season with salt, serve with chopped parsley for a garnish. The same recipe without fennel but with a little packet of saffron is called risotto milanese, though you can also use frutti di mare or whatever you have.

Risotto

Recipe type: Entrée Prep time: 10 mins Cook time: 30 mins   Total time: 40 mins

This fabulous rice dish is made in lots of different ways - here's a basic one. The idea with risotto is to add broth slowly to rice that's already been heated up, and to stir often, to bring out some of the rice's starch. This will give it sort of a creamy texture.

Ingredients

- ➢ 1 liter of water
- ➢ 2 cubes of broth to boil
- ➢ 1½ cups of arborio rice
- ➢ cup of white wine
- ➢ chopped fennel bulb

Instructions

1. On a side burner, bring 1 liter of water with 2 cubes of broth to boil.

2. In a large frying pan, saute ½ onion, diced small, and 1 clove of garlic, minced.

3. Add 1½ cups of arborio rice to the frying pan after three minutes and stir frequently for a few minutes.

4. Pour in ½ cup of white wine (be careful of the steam), and then start adding the broth one cup at a time, stirring continuously.

5. After several minutes, add ½ chopped fennel bulb. Keep stirring and adding broth until the rice is cooked.

6. Season with salt, serve with chopped parsley for a garnish. The same recipe without fennel but with a little packet of saffron is called risotto milanese, though you can also use frutti di mare or whatever you have.

Polenta

Polenta is a northern Italian classic, so much so that southern Italians call northerners "polentoni." It's essentially ground corn meal. Bring 3 cups of water to a boil in a large pot, with 1 broth cube in it. When it boils, pour in 1 cup of polenta, reduce heat, and stir vigorously and continuously for about ten minutes or until the polenta is thick. Put a nice slice of gorgonzola cheese on each plate, spoon the polenta over to melt it, then pour your favorite tomato sauce over the top. Cheap and very filling, it's a perfect meal for students. Make sure to get the polenta flour that says "cotta a vapore" or "cuoce in minuti": this is the precooked polenta flour. If not, you'll stir for 40-50 minutes this will put hair on your chest!

Polenta

Prep time: 5 mins   Cook time: 5 mins   Total time: 10 mins

Polenta is a northern Italian classic, so much so that southern Italians call northerners "polentoni." It's essentially ground corn meal. Cheap and very filling, it's a perfect meal for students. Make sure to get the polenta flour that says "cotta a vapore" or "cuoce in minuti": this is the precooked polenta flour. If not, you'll stir for 40-50 minutes this will put hair on your chest!

Ingredients

- ➢ A box of precooked polenta flour
- ➢ Water
- ➢ A box of Gorgonzola (you can even use just red souce)

Instructions

1. Bring 3 cups of water to a boil in a large pot, with 1 broth cube in it.

2. When it boils, pour in 1 cup of polenta, reduce heat, and stir vigorously and continuously for about ten minutes or until the polenta is thick.

3. Put a nice slice of gorgonzola cheese on each plate, spoon the polenta over to melt it, then pour your favorite tomato sauce over the top.

Spaghettini ai frutti di mare

Umbria is the only region on the peninsula that doesn't touch the sea, but you can still get great seafood at the Mercato coperto. This is Franci's recipe: in a large frying pan sautee but don't burn 3 cloves garlic, and a small white onion cut finely with 1C olive oil. Wash and clean 250g vongole (clams), 250g cozze (mussels), 200g kalamari, and 1 scampo (shrimp tail) for each person. When the onion is soft, add the seafood, reduce heat, and cover the frying pan. After five minutes, add 1 glass white wine and re-cover. After five more minutes, remove from heat, shell half the clams and mussels, cut fine, and put back in. Return to heat, add 3 large tomatoes cut small, a little bit of peperoncino, and a little black pepper. If all the water evaporates, add a bit. Cook 500g of spaghettini al dente, drain, and add to the frying pan. Stir well, put some finely cut garlic and parsley over the top, and serve.

Spaghettini ai frutti di mare

Prep time: 15 mins Cook time: 20 mins Total time: 35 mins

Umbria is the only region on the peninsula that doesn't touch the sea, but you can still get great seafood at the Mercato coperto.This is Franci's recipe:

Ingredients

- ➢ 500g of Spaghettini
- ➢ 3 cloves of garlic
- ➢ 1 small white onion
- ➢ 2 spoons of olive oil
- ➢ 250g of clams (vongole)
- ➢ 250 g mussels (cozze)
- ➢ 200 g kalamari
- ➢ 5 shrimps
- ➢ 1 glass of white wine
- ➢ 3 large tomatoes
- ➢ spices (black pepper and hot pepper)
- ➢ Parsley

Instructions

1. In a large frying pan sautee but don't burn 3 cloves garlic, and a small white onion cut finely with 1C olive oil.

2. Wash and clean 250g vongole (clams), 250g cozze (mussels), 200g kalamari, and 1 scampo (shrimp tail) for each person.

3. When the onion is soft, add the seafood, reduce heat, and cover the frying pan.

4. After five minutes, add 1 glass white wine and re-cover.

5. After five more minutes, remove from heat, shell half the clams and mussels, cut fine, and put back in.

6. Return to heat, add 3 large tomatoes cut small, a little bit of peperoncino, and a little black pepper.

7. If all the water evaporates, add a bit.

8. Cook 500g of spaghettini al dente, drain, and add to the frying pan.

9. Stir well, put some finely cut garlic and parsley over the top, and serve.

Shopping

You're going to want some memories of Perugia other than those on your head and in your scrapbook- here are our suggestions. Note that while Alan and I put in some of our favorites, this chapter was substantially written by Kathleen Heil, our shopping guru, and updated by our other intrepid shopper, Lauren Sinnott. Hard to believe, but Alan and I don't "love thread" and we aren't currently "lusting after the tan cashmere blend turtleneck sweater," though we understand those who are.

Ahh, shopping. Most of the stores in this section are in the center of Perugia, though some are at one of the two malls. The main mall, or Centro Commerciale is in Collestrada, about forty minutes away by bus. Take bus Q2, which leaves at 32 after the hour from Pallazzo Gallenga and from the mall at 19 after the hour. The main attractions there are the IperCoop (wow, a big supermarket), Zara, and Media World. The buses are few and far between so check the schedule before you leave and when you get off. There's also a big mall out in Ellera take bus Z4 from Piazza Partigiani to the Ellera Supermercato.

Another shopping note: Beware that except for a few of the larger chain stores that are orario non-stop, most shops close in the afternoon for la *pausa*, typically closing around 13:00 and reopening around 16:00. By the way, most shops in Italy are happy to gift wrap your purchase for you at no additional cost. Say "E' un regalo, potete incartarlo per favore?"

A Guide to Shopping in Perugia

Okay, so I know we're all abroad and on a budget…but, who doesn't want to take a little "pick-me-up" shopping trip once in awhile (every girl has got to get her fix!)? If you're looking for some shopping on a student budget, we have some tips to keep your wallet heavy and your arms filled with purchases!

Let's start with the two European stores that we all know and love: H&M and Zara (sorry, no Top Shop in this part of Italy!). These two moderately priced men's and women's fashion companies can be found at the Centro Commerciale Collestrada (also known as, "the mall"), which is about 40 minutes away from the Centro Storico by bus.

If you're not quite in the mood to make the trek to the mall, the center of Perugia also has its fair share of stores to browse around. Some of our favorites for affordable women's clothing include:

Contrasto > (on Via Calderini, just off of Corso Vannucci), a small boutique with trendy and colorful tops, shoes, coats, and costume jewelry;

Brandy Melville > (on Corso Vannucci), a California-inspired company with great single-sized basics;

Subdued > (on Via Baglioni, just off of Via Mazzini Giuseppe), a slightly pricier (but very hip!) Italian chain that includes all clothing pieces, tons of denim, and both lacey and studded items;

Kookai > Across from Niba at Maestà delle Volte 1 is this French import with the latest trends for women. I'm currently lusting after the tan cashmere blend turtleneck sweater with the leather elbow patches and the embroidered gnome. Skirts, sweaters, jackets and shirts from €30-250.

<u>18 MQ</u> > (on Via dei Priori), a VERY small shop with BIG clothing finds;

<u>Strangers' Corner</u> > in Piazza Cavallotti (just behind the bus stop near Piazza Morlacchi) for splurges on funky jewelry;

<u>United Colors of Benetton</u> > You would never know it from looking at the bland rows of clothing on the walls but this ubiquitous Italian chain was once infamous for its print ads, which used controversial images of drug addicts and Jesus. Nothing special these days, but if you're in dire need of a generic sweater and it's *la pausa* time, Benetton will do. Mo-Sa 10-20:00.

...and finally, a <u>small vintage shop</u> (on Via Luigi Masi, across from the RAI building just above the bus station in Piazza Partigiani) with adorable used tops, bags, and accessories from the past.

So, next time you're feeling a *little blue* in Perugia...give yourself a *little pink* treat and explore the shops around the town! After all, shopping therapy nearly always does the trick in Italy.

As far as <u>men's shopping goes</u>, you cannot go wrong at <u>Sisley</u> (on Via Mazzini) for hard-wearing tops and bottoms;

<u>Smooth Kicks</u> **>** (near Via delle Rupe) provides a large collection of sneakers and other (quite flashy!) shoes;

And, for those guys and girls looking to find sports gear within a short walking distance from the Center, try <u>Coni Sport</u> (under the big arches toward Piazza Morlacchi) for sneakers and "big name" sports brands, like Adidas.

AC Perugia soccer clothing > You can easily buy online some Perugia soccer merchandising . But if you want to try it on and browse then you have to go at "Calcio Mania" at Centro Commerciale Gherlinda (Via Pierluigi Nervi, 5 06073 Corciano). Take the G1 bus from Piazza Italia and ask the bus driver to stop at Gherlinda (double check on umbriamobilita.it).

Party Costumes > You will probably have occasion at least once to put on a costume while you're in Perugia. One place to get costumes and other party stuff is Divertilandia, down by the station at Via Campo di Marte 10e. Take buses G or A down from Piazza Partigiani, or, standing in front of the station, walk along the big street to the right until you see it on the left. The phone is 075. 505.6704 and the hours are standard.

<u>Coni Sport</u> **>** An extensive and well-priced selection of the hottest American and European brands in sneakers and sportswear. Converse, Vans, Nike, Jack Jones, Nordicapp, Adidas, and Puma, to name just a few. Check out the back wall on the right for bargains they sometimes have Pumas on clearance for as little as €30. At Maesta delle Volte, 16. Walk from bar Centrale (on Piazza IV Novembre) straight past the steps and go straight until you are in Via Maestà delle Volte, then angle down right. Follow this winding street till you see Coni in the corner. Mo-Sa 9:20-13, 15-20:00 and Sun 11-20:00.

Directions to Centro Commerciale Collestrada

To arrive at the Centro Commerciale Collestrada, take the Q2 city bus from Piazza Morlacchi towards Collestrada Centro Commerciale. Remember to allow plenty of leeway time for bus delays, stops, and general mishaps; we suggest leaving about an hour and twenty minutes for total travel time, just to be safe. Also, keep in mind that the mall is generally closed on Sundays and its bus line does not run on those days, either. If Sunday is your only option for mall travel, though, you can check out the frequently updated Collestrada site, which can be easily translated into English. Once you have arrived at the mall, feel free to browse around the two large clothing stores, but keep in mind that the Centro Commerciale closes at 9:00 PM every day, except for Fridays (when it closes at 10:00 PM). In addition to H&M and Zara, the Centro Commerciale also boasts a huge Ipercoop, which has the biggest and best grocery sales, and a gelato shop with some of the creamiest ice cream around!

Typical Products

A directory of stores where you can find typical products.

<u>L'arte dei Vasai ></u> Umbria is known for its pottery, and at the shop in Via Baglioni, L'arte dei Vasai, there are lots of nice gifts to take home. As they say in their ad, their items "differ only in price and size, not in workmanship." You can even ask them to personalize something for you, like a plate or a perfect ceramic Christmas tree ornament. They are open normal business hours and can ship their beautiful creations home, wherever home is. Skip the long trip to Deruta and just take a stroll down Via Baglioni 32, 075.971.1284.

<u>Sardegna e Sapori ></u> You don't need to take the slow boat to Sardegna to get your obscure prodotti tipici fix. Facing the Tre Archi simply turn left on Corso Cavour and head to 107 for traditional wine, cheese, and breads from my favorite Italian island

in a sweet little shop. Wines and cheeses, about 6, breads about 3. 10-20:30, Mo-Sa and 11-20:00 Su.

OlivoIdea > On the cold, shady side of the cathedral, just above where Via Ulisse Rocchi ends. This shop has all sorts of cool things made out of olive wood, the perfect gift to take home and which won't break in your backpack. Friendly Robert is ready to help you in English, Italian, or German. Open 10:45-19:30, closed Sunday and Monday morning. Takes Visa and MC.

Talmone > At 12 Maesta delle Volte on the way down to Piazza Morlacchi is a shop that sells carrots, CDs, sausages and mushrooms...all made of chocolate. If the novelty of eating a sweet that resembles a vegetable is lost on you and your loved ones, buy some truffles instead. Visa, MasterCard.

Phones, Electronics, Computers

Telefonini > Cell phones in Italy are called "telefonini," the affectionate diminutive of the word for phone. It should be an affectionate word as people sometimes seem to love their telefonini more than their relatives. Anyway, I wish I could give advice on which one is the best. My first year here we measured this by how far from the windows of our apartment we could be and still have coverage, but this changes year to year. Kate says Wind* means you have to be outside in a breeze to get reception! Try the friendly (English-speaking) Luca at the Vodafone store in Piazza Danti behind the Duomo near the fountain.

Mediaworld > A massive electronamagic store which is at the Collestrada mall.

Stationery and Art Supplies

Photocopies > I recommend the place that printed a previous edition of this guide, the Psycopisteria at Via Baldeschi 7 (it runs from Piazza Cavalotti to Via Ulisse Rocchi). There the slightly psycho Alfonso will make you black and white or color photocopies, do digital transfer, and all your other *copisteria* wishes. It's open 9:30-19:00 with the lunch break, though Al sometimes leaves early to teach shiatsu or read Ginsberg at Caffè Morlacchi.

Art Deco > If you are already an artist, you may need supplies try at this store at the bottom of Via dei Priori, number 93. It wasn't set in stone at the time of press but the owner may give a discount with the EG card. Show it to her and cross your fingers!

Magazzini Rastelli > Photocopies, school/office supplies, and a limited selection of your basic art supplies can be found at the bottom of Via

Baglioni, 21. Pick up a Teenage Mutant Ninja Turtles notebook for €1 here and then head next door to the other outpost, where you can continue to mourn your lost youth amidst a random selection of stuffed animals and toys.

<u>Film & Photographic Paper</u> > All your photo needs can be taken care of by the sweet and cultured Daniela at Foto Color, Via dei Priori 1. See the entry for Developing Film in <u>Perugia: A-Z</u>.

Apartment Needs

Once you find a room (we hope you did) here is where you come!

<u>Secondhand</u> > If you are in Perugia for a short time and a good time you probably won't need to buy much in the way of furniture. Almost all rooms and apartments are let furnished. There are a few tiny secondhand shops in the central city area but their

stuff is mainly antiques and priced accordingly. A good range of affordable furnishings and more (everything from entire kitchens to clothes and DVD's) is to be found at the Moby Dick stores. The two local branches are at Via Eugubina 111f (open 9:30-12:30 & 15:30-19:30 Tu-Sa) and the other at Via dei Filosofi 76n (in a basement, open 15:30-19:30 Mo-Sa). Take the ever-necessary documento with you because you will need some personal identification if you wish to purchase anything. No, they don't have used whales; try Norway.

Hardware Store > Occasionally you will need something like nails, screws, cords, bulbs, tools, keys, etc. There are several ferramenta around the center but the one where Zach gets all his twine, drill bits, and charcoal is at Via Ulisse Rocchi 17. Man-of-steel Luigi will be happy to help you find what you need, and maybe teach you a word of Perugian dialect. Oh, and check out his pictures from the weightlifting days back by the cash register; he's also a personal trainer if you need one! If you live in the down part of the city, there's Ferramenta Severi at Corso Cavour 36. For those who end up living in a shared house with only one coffee cup, yes, they do have kitchenwares as well. Most hardware stores are closed Saturday afternoon. For do-it-your-selfers, there's SELF in Via Pallotta near the Via Filosofi intersection. It has a large selection of tools and housewares and is open Mo-Sa 9-13:00 and 15:30-20:00. 075.322.20. Take any of the E buses from Piazza Partigiani, then get off just after the bus turns into Via della Palotta. SELF is on the other side of the street.

Osram > Lots of useful little appliances, like irons, desk lamps, and hair dryers can be found here at 16 Via dei Priori, just past the Diesel store. Or, if you're looking for something useless, they sell an electric cotton candy maker here, too.

<u>Convenineza Casa</u>> It has two levels, the first one has a lot of stuff from detergents to notebooks and the one above is for home supplies. It is located just at the beginning (if you come from Piazza Fortebraccio) of via Fabretti. Very affordable!

<u>Conti</u> > There's a sign behind the cash register that says, "Conti just about everything." Yep, that's true. It's on Piazza Matteotti near the Coop; they have clothes downstairs and all sorts of housewares upstairs. It's the best place to go before an improvised party in your cramped student apartment you can get ten tea candles, a new salad bowl, a serving spoon, and six plastic water cups (also great for vino) for about €9.

<u>Upim</u> > Just above the Coop at the train station. A great place for basic clothes, towels, and kitchen, things like that. Lauren says that most of her bathroom apparel and such is from Upim.

Housewares PG > Not the real name but that's what we call it. It's at Via Bartolo 19-21 near Quattro Passi. The nice ladies there will help you find some inexpensive water glasses, a nutcracker, a big plastic bowl, or whatever else you need for that big dinner. Perugino lessons are free with any purchase!

Gifts

Ceramics > Majolic pottery is probably the most common gift to take back home. See L'arte dei Vasai above in the Prodotti Tipici section.

Le Folli Fate > In Italian, when you graduate, you *laurearti*, you laurel yourself. That's why you see the students in nice clothes with that laurel wreath around their heads they've just graduated. We're not so sentimental but we think that a great souvenir to take home with you is a laurel wreath. Drop by Le Folli Fate at Via Ulisse Rochi 14 from

Tuesday to Saturday, 9-12:30 & 16-19:30, and ask for helpful Nadia.

<u>Monimbò</u> > You'll need a present for a birthday or going-away party sooner or later. I'd suggest Cooperativa Monimbò, a great little store that has "fair trade" (as opposed to so-called "free trade") goods, where the producers in the Third World get a much higher share of the final price. Go there for great coffee, tea, chocolate, rice, spices, snacks, lots of handcrafts excellent for presents and plenty of feel-good philosophy. It's at Via Bonazzi 41a, just down the stairs that are next to the *biglietteria* for the buses on Piazza Italia.

<u>Musica Musica</u> > Mom might appreciate the great Italian tenor Andrea Boccelli...or maybe Jiovanotti is more her style. In any event, go the nobleman's stables-turned-music store and the magic Fofo will

help you pick out some tunes. It's at Via Oberdan 51.

Olivoldea > Like things made out of olive wood?

Il Telaio > Horrified by the prospect of breaking a bottle of olive oil in your luggage on the way home? Il Telaio has gorgeous, traditional Umbrian fabrics woven by the same family for well over a hundred years. Signora Adagatti will be happy to show you her range of original and typical designs all done in classical Umbrian style. Once upon a time real rust was used for the red color in Perugian designs but nowadays the regime of washing machines and fabric softener requires more durable artificial colors. The textiles are on the expensive side but looking and appreciating is well and truly free. Open 9:30-13:00 & 16:30-19:30 Tu-Sat at Via Ulisse Rocchi 19.

Olive Oil > Oil crisis? Peak Oil? Italy's most over-rated food product, though at least a passable door lubricant, can be bought in bulk direct from cottage industries that press the olives themselves. The nearest is probably Antico Frantoio Trampolini at Via del Giochetto 103, a twenty minute walk from Prosciutti. They also have a lot of great specialty oils and vinegars (balsamic vinegar *al ciocolato*) and if you have a big enough group, will do tastings and demonstrations. Open 7:30-13:00 & 14:30-19:00 daily except Sundays.

Antiques > The antique market is held at the end of the month in Piazza Italia and surrounds. Apart from antique furniture (everything from bedside tables to grand pianos) there are usually secondhand books, prints and etchings, household goods and all kinds of knick knacks. If you really need a plaster bust of Mussolini this is the place to be. Early morning until sunset, last Saturday and Sunday of every month.

Leather Journals > Antonio is our man out by the Duomo — he handmakes all of his wares. You can also drop by the cool place in Via Guardabassi, before Passion Tattoo on the other side of the street. A great place for your Perugia memories.

Other

Other random things you may need.
Sementi Rosi > Have a garden and want to plant some plants or seeds? Sementi Rosi can help, and you might even see Dave there. They're just up above the bar right on the corner at Porta Pesa. They also have pet food for those of you who have small animals living with you.

Ticchioni Sport > Another place with clothes but also sporting and outdoors equipment. It's a busride away, at Via XX Settembre 73, near the

Banca dei Monti dei Paschi di Siena. 075.500.6870. You're looking for a decent backpack, right? Well unfortunately you probably won't find it there.

<u>Sexy Shop</u> > You may have need of "marital aids" while you're here, and the only place is in San Sisto. Take bus R from Piazza Italia and get off about twenty minutes later in front of the Perugina factory. Cross the huge field behind the shopping center and look for a building on the right of the BMW dealership. Go around the side for a wide selection of adult materials, including a prophylactic special for those who have studied The (Non) Dating Guide: €18 for one hundred and forty-four condoms.

Cultural Activities

Life in Perugia has a lot to offer other than studying Italian and meeting people from all over the world!   Here you can find some cultural distractions.

Cinema >: In the historical center of Perugia we have now four small cinemas.

Cinema Sant'Angelo in Corso Garibaldi soldiers on: head up Corso Garibaldi to #97 and hang your next right in Via Lucida. For movie info call 075.448.77 or even better look at www.cinegatti.it.

UCI Cinema (Borgonovo mall) is outside the center.: It's about a twenty minute ride, and you can ask the bus driver to let you off at the *Centro Borgonovo*, though it's hard to miss. Make sure you check the schedule for returning buses, or you'll have to take a taxi after the movie. Note too that like almost everywhere in provincial Italy, all films are dubbed into Italian. The Space cinema is another movie theater is just a bit outside Perugia inside the Gherlinda mall in Corciano-Perugia, huge screens and drink holder; you want the G1 bus from Piazza Italia.

During the summer there are also movies in the open-air theater in the Frontone Gardens, across from San Pietro at the end of Corso Cavour (where it's called Borgo XX Giugno).

Literature >: Bookstores with foreign books are abundant, though they don't all have fantastic selections. Check out La Feltrinelli in Corso Vannucci, Grimana Libri across from the Stranieri, and L'Altra Libreria in Via Ulisse Rocchi. They all have Zach's two mysteries, *Peril in Perugia* and *Death by Chocolate* (see his shameless description in the "Perugia Personalities" section). Here at Little Blue, we can recommend a number of good books about Italy, but most of them are hard to find in Perugia. The exception is *Fire on Mount Maggiore*, a thriller by John Parras, which you can find at the Feltrinelli. The Augusta Library (a

223

minute's walk from the fountain) is a good place to study in silence and to read. Go up Via del Sole from just behind the Duomo, then straight on Via Delle Prome and the library is almost at the end of the street on the right.

Another one we can recommend is *Home Street Home: Perugia's History Told Through Its Streets.* Far from being another boring tourist guide, this book tells about Perugia's past by describing what happened in each street. Learn about Pig Street, Bride Street, and Piazza Grimana.

Drama >: You've probably had your share already (see the "(Non) Dating Guide") but if you want to simply watch it, you have a few choices. The main theater in town is Teatro Morlacchi, which has good student rates, but there's also Teatro Sant'Angelo (in a sidestreet off Corso Garibaldi). Once again, to make it worthwhile you need to know Italian decently well.

If you're not yet convinced that living in Italy for a while will turn you into a raving drama queen, you can participate in the Human Beings theater group. HB has been running for twelve years and brings together people from different countries and backgrounds to explore their creative potential. At some times of the year they do workshops only, while at others they work towards a public performance piece. Contact resident director Danilo at 349.861.8557 or visit the site, www.humanbeings.it. If you decide to go, it's in the public school in Viale Roma, right after the Esso station. Enter, go down the hall, around to the right of the courtyard and down the stairwell.

Music >: Need some tunes? We go to Musica, Musica in Via Oberdan 51 (across from La Libreria, just before the steps), which has the best selection, new and used, cds and vinyl, and recent imports. It also used to be the stable of the palace of the Perugian nobleman who lived above it. It's open 9:30-20:00 every day except Sunday. Live music is pretty standard in pubs, so drop by your favorite watering hole or look for the ubiquitous flyers around town. Italian airwaves are jam-packed with stations so you are certainly not stuck for choice. State-run radio 3 is pretty austere but worth consideration by those who seek a solid model for spoken Italian. Radio Subasio is king of the local stations with wall-to-wall pop. Want to hear great lectures about music? Check the Uni per Stranieri schedules for the Storia della Musica lectures (C1 and C2) of Professor Ragni, an excellent lecturer. He often has unregistered "visitors" in his class, so drop by. He also gives concerts.

Classical music concerts are occasionally put on by the comune for free, and inexpensively by the Fondazione Perugia Musica Classica, also called "*amici della Musica*." As usual, this year there will be a lot of world-class concerts, with international-level talent. The concerts will be held here in Perugia in venues like San Pietro, San Domenico, and of course the stunnng Teatro Morlacchi. Their office is in Via Danzetta 7 (a sidestreet of Corso Vannucci): Just ring the bell and go up to the second floor, the employees are friendly and eager to please. Get a program there or look on the site, www.perugiamusicaclassica.com, for more details. You can also call 075.572.2271.

The End